JACOBY
ON
BRIDGE

"If you want to improve your game, *JACOBY ON BRIDGE* will prove to be an ideal teacher."
—*Cleveland Plain Dealer*

———————————

JAMES JACOBY is one of the world's greatest bridge players. He co-authored his father's (the late Oswald Jacoby) newspaper column on bridge for many years and continues it today. His column now appears in more than 600 newspapers nationwide and is the most popular of its kind. Jim, who co-authored *JACOBY ON CARD GAMES* with his father, continues to play (and win) on the world-class bridge circuit. His record includes two World Championships and sixteen North American Championships, including two Grand National Teams and three Reisinger Board-a-Match Teams.

Books by James Jacoby

Jacoby on Bridge
Jacoby on Card Games
  (with Oswald Jacoby)

Published by POCKET BOOKS

JACOBY
ON
BRIDGE

James Jacoby

POCKET BOOKS

New York   London   Toronto   Sydney   Tokyo

POCKET BOOKS, a division of Simon & Schuster Inc.
1230 Avenue of the Americas, New York, NY 10020

Copyright © 1987 by James Jacoby
Cover photo copyright © 1989 Mort Engel

Published by arrangement with Pharos Books
Library of Congress Catalog Card Number: 87-60160

ISBN: 0-671-66884-6

First Pocket Books printing December 1989

10 9 8 7 6 5 4 3 2 1

POCKET and colophon are registered trademarks
of Simon & Schuster Inc.

Printed in the U.S.A.

Dedication

From the time the Jacoby name became synonymous with bridge there was one most diligent critic. She did her best to make sure that every "i" was dotted and every "t" crossed. Needless to say, it was largely due to her efforts that each suit has 13 cards and every diagrammed deal makes sense. With love and gratitude I dedicate this book to my mother.

Mary Zita Jacoby
(Mary Zita Jacoby died on May 14, 1987.)

Acknowledgments

I wish to express my thanks to Frank Stewart, associate editor of the *Contract Bridge Bulletin,* for his suggestions and his assistance in preparing the biographical material on Oswald Jacoby. My thanks also to Richard Bass, who edited the final manuscript.

Contents

Contents

Contents

Contents

Part Two:
THE PLAY OF THE CARDS

Part Three:
SAMPLE HANDS

Contents

Preface
Indomitable Oswald Jacoby
(1902–1984)

The time is February, 1929. Wall Street's plunge is still eight months away, and a carefree America is pursuing its leisure time in various passionate ways. Contract bridge, invented only three years earlier, has become a rage, inexorably supplanting auction bridge. Now the Knickerbocker Whist Club of New York City has decided to hold the first big contract tournament, the Eastern Championships Goldman Pairs. The winner is a relative unknown—a full-bodied, ebullient young man of 26, with dark, curly hair and a remarkable, computer-like mind. His partner is the Knickerbocker's chairman, an old lion of auction days named George Reith. Reith has pressed him into service at the last minute, having forgotten to get himself a partner in his rush to organize the event. The legend of Oswald Jacoby is sown.

Fifty-five years later. December 4, 1983. A ballroom at the Sheraton Bal Harbour, Miami Beach. A thin, curling haze of cigarette smoke floats above the long rows of card tables, adding substance to an already tense atmosphere. The Reisinger Board-a-Match Teams, perhaps the most strenuous of the North American Championships conducted by the American Contract Bridge League, is reaching its climax. Every player knows that one slip can mean the loss of a hand and perhaps the tournament.

In the middle of the ballroom sits an older gentleman. His thinning shock of white hair bears witness to his age; not so, his sparkling eyes and alert demeanor. His gestures are frequent and animated. The aura of restless energy that surrounds him and sets him apart from the other players can be sensed from a vantage point far across the big room. Oswald Jacoby has come once more to play—and triumph—in the intensely competitive world of tournament bridge that he loves.

My father was born in Brooklyn on December 8, 1902. He played his first bridge with family and friends at the age of ten. At fifteen, he somehow conned himself into the army, saw two months' service in World War I and was awarded the Victory Medal. Mathematics was a family interest, so when Oswald enrolled at Columbia University, he chose math as his major. A famous story from his college days shows that his prodigious mental powers were already in full flight. In physics class the instructor posed a complex problem in ballistics. Jacoby challenged his mentor's answer and was reprimanded. But later the instructor found that his prepared answer was wrong while the one Jacoby had come up with in his head was correct. It was not the last time Ozzie would delight in testing his mental prowess.

Jacoby left Columbia after two years and went to work for the Metropolitan Life Insurance Company. There he amazed everyone by passing the Society of Actuaries' exams at the age of twenty-one, at that time the youngest ever to do so. He always maintained he could have done it at twenty.

In college Jacoby had been involved in a number of extracurricular pursuits, and he soon began his long string of successes at bridge. Then, in 1931, came an event that thrust him squarely into the public eye. The contract frenzy was reaching its climax. Ely Culbertson and a group of experts led by Sidney Lenz were vying for the patronage of the bridge-playing public. Culbertson issued a challenge to a set match, which Lenz eventually had to accept. Jacoby's brilliance was so well-known in the upper echelons of the game that Lenz, an established star, chose him for his partner over a number of more prominent experts.

The partnership, however, was ill-fated. Jacoby's penchant for daring bluff bids on nonexistent values confused the stodgy Lenz as well as his opponents, and recriminations were inevitable. Finally, two-thirds of the way through the match, Jacoby penned a gracious letter of withdrawal and another player carried on in his place. But his "psychic" bids and psychologically brilliant plays had captured the public's imagination, and his individualism and daring exploits at the table inevitably made him a permanent public favorite to rival the mercurial Culbertson.

Jacoby went on to become the most successful tournament player in the country in the thirties. In 1935, his team, the Four Horsemen, defeated a French squad to win the first official World Team Championship of bridge. Later he became a member of the famous Four Aces team, continuing to win everything in sight.

On December 7, 1941, ten years to the day after the Culbertson-Lenz match had begun, Jacoby and B.J. Becker were leading a national championship event in Richmond, Virginia, when word came of Pearl Harbor. Jacoby rose from the table, packed his bags, and left for the war—he did not play bridge again for four years. Involved in counterintelligence and cryptanalysis, he helped break German and Japanese codes.

Years later, when the Korean War broke out, my father received a telephone call from Washington—a computer was needed in the Far East. "Buy one," Jacoby said. "We can't buy one. You're the one," was the reply. A week later, at considerable personal sacrifice, Jacoby found himself in Japan, again engaged in counterintelligence.

When Jacoby returned from his third stint in the military, he found that Charles Goren had overtaken him as the ACBL's leading masterpoint holder. He quickly determined to recapture the top spot. Four times in the years from 1959 to 1963, he won the McKenney Trophy for most masterpoints earned in one year. He was the first player to win a thousand points in a single year, and in 1967 he became the first to win ten thousand points overall. Until he voluntarily curtailed his tournament activity, he was the league's top masterpoint holder.

From 1969 to 1971 Jacoby served as nonplaying captain of the United States International Team. In 1970 and again in 1971, the U.S. team managed to win the Bermuda Bowl, symbol of the World Championship, for the first time since the early fifties.

Jacoby was a man for all seasons. He lectured on probability theory at M.I.T. and wrote books on mathematics. He was for six years a member of the Board of Visitors of Harvard Observatory. Before the 1929 crash he enjoyed sizable gains in the stock market. He remained an actuarial consultant. He was a computer expert, a friend of four presidents, an ardent patriot.

Yet he focused his brilliance and erudition principally on games. He won the world backgammon championship, was an expert poker player, and made a formidable opponent at any two-handed card game—canasta, for instance—because he automatically remembered all the outstanding cards. In addition, he was a chess player good enough to beat United States Champion Frank Marshall in college and to get a draw with Tigran Petrosian when the then world champion spotted him a knight in a 1963 rapid-transit game. (Chess experts who watched this game were amazed. "It's unbelievable," said one. "Lightning chess is Petrosian's best game.") Throughout his life, you could name your game and Jacoby would beat you at it.

Although he played many kinds of card games and published best-selling books about them, it was for bridge that he displayed an unparalleled aptitude. My father had more attributes of a big winner at bridge than anyone else. "He's good at so many things that go into being a bridge player," columnist Alfred Sheinwold once said. The tournament game was the perfect arena for him, with his Olympian self-assurance, dynamic temperament, and love of competition. His remarkable aptitude for the game was exhibited in the many technical innovations that he pioneered. Ozzie became the Edison of bridge, developing many bidding methods that are part of almost every modern tournament player's arsenal.

His mind was perhaps the quickest of all time (and it remained so when, in the end, his body had declined). "He had," expert Edgar Kaplan says, "the fastest mind of any man I ever met." Ozzie could multiply two six-digit numbers in his head. He solved problems, both in logic and mathematics, like lightning. His mind, in fact, was apt to outrace tongue and pen. Few could decipher his handwriting, and many listeners were baffled by his rapid-fire delivery when he spoke.

Although his speed of thought served him well at the bridge table, it meant that he often had to wait for others. "I must have spent six years of my life waiting for other people to finish games," he once grumbled. I can attest to that. My father didn't want to waste time. He wanted to get on to the next contest, the next hand, where there would be some new problem for him to think about.

His impatience was legendary—he once played gin rummy with the formidable John Crawford (and won) while simultaneously engaged in a hot bridge game. Especially frustrating for Ozzie were the times he became dummy—he developed a penchant for wandering away from the table rather than watch his partner's painstaking efforts. His habits became so widely known that, on one occasion, the playwright George S. Kaufman encountered him striding down Madison Avenue, midway between the two major bridge clubs in New York City. "Well, Ozzie, I know you're dummy somewhere," sighed Kaufman. "Is it at the Regency or the Cavendish?"

At the rarefied levels of national competition where all the players have talent, desire can be the decisive quality, and in this Jacoby was unsurpassed. Richard Frey, an old teammate, called Jacoby "a mercurial individual who had to be the best at everything and was the most intense person I've ever known." According to Kaplan, "He enjoyed nothing as much as winning." My mother, Mary Zita, said of him, "He didn't drink or smoke, yet he could get higher than a cloud over a game of old maid."

A 1935 story attests to my father's fierce fighting spirit. Laid up with a bad tooth, he wasn't expected to attend that year's national championships in Chicago. But as the tournament progressed and he read newspaper reports that western players were sweeping the events, sectional pride overcame him. Recruiting the late Eddie Hymes as his partner, Jacoby flew to Chicago and entered the open pairs event. He was deathly ill for three weeks after the trip, but he and Hymes captured the title.

No one enjoyed himself more at a bridge tournament. If you came upon an expert gathering, chances were that Jacoby would be right in the middle of it, laughing, gesticulating, and arguing vehemently.

In 1982 my mother and father celebrated their fiftieth anniversary. That same year, my father wrote his ten-thousandth bridge column for Newspaper Enterprise Association.

Jacoby was a member of the Bridge Hall of Fame and was an honorary World Bridge Federation Grand Master. In 1983, he was named the International Bridge Press Association's Personality of the Year. The award was presented at a special meeting of the IBPA at that year's World Championship in Stockholm. It was not generally known at this time that my father was fighting a deadly disease. I accepted the award on his behalf, with the following words:

"I am honored to accept this award for Oswald Jacoby. It is fitting that this award take place in Scandinavia, a land with a centuries-old tradition of warriors going to sea facing unknown foes. As some of you know, my father is now facing a most implacable enemy. He brings the same courage and joy of encounter to this battle that he has brought to every contest in eighty years. In this city, William Faulkner once said, 'Man's spirit shall prevail.' That statement is confirmed by what I am experiencing with my family. I thank all of you."

This was the restless, white-haired gentleman who sat playing bridge in the smoky ballroom in Miami Beach, pitting himself against a succession of players just half his age.

For two days, Jacoby's team played hard bridge just to reach the finals of this event. Now, for the first of the two final sessions, Jacoby has teamed up with Kaplan. The field is reduced to eleven teams, the elite of American bridgedom.

Since all the players are experts, absolute attention at the table is essential. Not a detail must be missed. But Jacoby's mind has seemed to grow sharper, if anything, with every passing year. As the famous British player Terence Reese wrote, long experience and assured technique preserve the stamina better than young legs. Concentrating fiercely and calling on his decades of experience, Jacoby helps engineer one good result after another. His team ends the afternoon with a tremendous score, good enough to vault them into contention with still one more session to go.

In the evening, Jacoby prowls the sidelines while his teammates—Kaplan, the tough Floridians Bill Root and Richard Pavlicek, and the great Philadelphian Norman Kay—battle to gain the lead the old man has put within their reach. The going is tough, and at the finish, the scores are breathtakingly close. But the team does win. And Jacoby has become the oldest player ever to win a major North American Championship, the twenty-seventh of his career. (He won eleven additional national championships before the formation of the ACBL.)

It is a remarkable moment in the history of American bridge and in the life of Oswald Jacoby. The whole tournament, more than five thousand bridge players, seems buoyed up with an uncharacteristic exhilaration. Even the most disappointed veterans are heard to say, "We didn't mind losing today."

In the press room, where a score of bridge journalists have assembled to cover the tournament, there is pandemonium. Jacoby seems to be the only dry-eyed person in the house—everyone knows that he will not defend his title. I rush in and hug him.

"Inviting Ozzie to play on our team was more a sentimental gesture than anything," Kaplan says. "He's been a very good friend to all of us. When I was a young man, he played a lot with me. We all wanted him to do well in this event, but we really didn't expect to win. And we surely didn't expect Ozzie to bring us in."

The team's score in the evening, without Jacoby, is well short of their stellar afternoon effort. "Ozzie," Kay says with a twinkle, "I know you're great, but I didn't think you were five winning deals better than me." The team's consensus—without Jacoby, victory would have slipped away.

When my father died in his longtime residence of Dallas on June 27, 1984, his career had spanned seven decades and he had left a compelling imprint on all seven. Tributes and reminiscences poured in from peers who felt a personal sense of loss. Perhaps the most fitting was from Alfred Sheinwold: "Oswald Jacoby made hundreds of friends," Sheinwold said, "and never lost a single one."

An era had ended. But as long as the game of bridge is played, Oswald Jacoby's name will be remembered with awe and affection.

PART ONE

THE
BIDDING

The object of bidding is to arrive at a slam, a game or a safe part-score contract when your side has the better cards, or to interfere with the opponents' exchange of information or to indicate the best defense when they have better cards.

A bidding *system* is the total extent of a partnership's agreements on what its bids and bidding sequences mean. An effective system should allow a player to accurately describe his hand to his partner in as few bids as possible.

Point Count

The high-card point count is a way of estimating the strength of a hand. It simplifies matters for the average player, and it is so accurate (especially for valuing balanced hands) that even experts use it habitually. No player, in fact, can afford to do without it. Here are tables showing the values:

High-card points:

Each ace	4 points
Each king	3 points
Each queen	2 points
Each jack	1 point

Distributional points:

To adjust for the extra value of long and short suits, points are added for distribution.

Each void suit	3 points
Each singleton . . :	2 points
Each doubleton	1 point

Add 1 point for each card beyond four in a suit that is so strong you don't need support in partner's hand to establish it. Examples of such suits are K Q J 9 3, A K J 4 3, A K 8 6 4 2 and A Q 10 9 4 2.

Subtract 1 point for 4-3-3-3 distribution. THIS IS MOST IMPORTANT.

Distributional points normally are counted only in suit bidding. However, long cards may readily be established in no-trump play.

Here are some key numbers to remember.

Strength in the combined hands needed for:

Grand slam (all 13 tricks)	37 points
Small slam (12 tricks)	33 points
Minor suit game (11 tricks)	29 points
Major suit game (10 tricks)	26 points
No-trump game (9 tricks)	26 points

WORKING POINTS

It's adequate to use point count with no adjustments when you are trying for a part-score or game and the opponents aren't bidding. Twenty-six points usually will produce game in no-trump or, if a fit is found, in a major suit. Twenty-five points or less will only be enough for a part-score. If you follow this rule, you will be a reasonably successful bidder.

When you get to slams in no-trump, 33 high-card points for a small slam or 37 for a grand slam should be enough. If you have 33 HCP, it is impossible for the opponents to hold two aces. If you have 37 HCP, they can't have even one ace.

In suit slams you will be counting points for distribution, so that two aces may well be missing even though your total is 33 points or more. You can avoid reaching a slam missing two aces by using the Blackwood convention—see page 118.

There is another point to remember about slam bidding—aces, kings, singletons, and voids are *working points* when you are in the slam zone. Queens, jacks, and small doubletons also may have value, but they are not pulling their full weight in slam country. (In truth, queens and jacks are slightly overvalued on the 4-3-2-1 scale, particularly for suit play.) A holding like a small tripleton is a bad sign for slam purposes—unless partner has all three top honors, there may be a loser in the suit.

Therefore, when you start thinking about a slam, *look at the workers.* Pay less attention to queens and jacks unless they lie in a suit you expect to use for tricks. Be wary when you can't take the first or second lead of a dangerous-looking suit. Be aggressive when you have first- or second-round control of all four suits.

COMPETITIVE JUDGMENT

Counting points can tell you the approximate trick-taking power of the hands, but points still do not take tricks—high cards, long cards, and trumps do. You must not bid in a vacuum. In competitive situations you must realize that some points will become worthless, while others will increase in value.

In competition at or above game-level, you always should look at your cards in an enemy suit from the standpoint of *how many tricks you will lose as declarer* and of *how many tricks you will take on defense.*

There is an easy way to value a doubleton (even one that includes the queen)—just count it as two losing tricks. A holding of three small cards is a trifle better—if both opponents have bid the suit vigorously, there is a good chance partner will have a singleton, reducing your three losing tricks to one. Bear in mind, however, that it is dangerous to value your partner's hand for him. If your partner is, in fact, looking at a singleton, he should know how to value it and how much higher your side should bid.

How about K-x in an enemy suit? If you believe that the ace is to your right, the king will become a sure trick either on offense or defense. If you think the ace is to your left, the king becomes worthless on defense. It could be valuable on offense, but only if you are declarer—in this case the enemy cannot attack the suit right away without letting you score the king.

Thus, a guarded king may be a working card, but queens and jacks in the enemy's suit probably are worth nothing for offense.

TENS AND NINES

Tens and nines are assigned no point value, but they are important cards nonetheless, especially for play in no-trump. They help your high cards in the suit develop tricks, and they tend to cut down on the number of tricks the opponents can take there. When a 10 or a 10-9 combination backs up a jack, those spots can be worth their weight in gold.

The term *body* refers to your overall spot-card holdings, and particularly your spots in the suits you are bidding. K Q 10 9 8 of trumps probably will produce four tricks and surely will produce three; K Q 4 3 2 may bring in the same three or four tricks, but it also may take just one.

Suppose, at no-trump, you hold J 10 9 2 of a suit. You may never establish the jack for a trick, but it is a lead-pipe cinch that the opponents won't take four tricks against you. If your partner has, say, Q 6, you are sure to take two tricks if you have time to knock out the opponents' ace and king.

Give your partner A 6 4. You can lead the jack for a finesse and, if it loses, lead the ten for a second finesse. Unless the king and queen both lie behind the ace, you can neutralize one of those two cards.

Now change your holding to J 5 4 3. Opposite Q 6 you can never take more than one trick in the suit, and you may not take any. Opposite A 6 4 your chances for two tricks aren't nearly as good.

How do you value tens and nines as working points? Look your hand over. One ten and one nine is average. If you have a choice between a bid and a pass, bid when you have more than your fair share of the high spots (especially when they reside in *your* long suits and not the enemy's). Pass when you have fewer high spots than normal.

Body is most important in competitive situations, where good spot-cards in your long suits may well turn out to be especially valuable.

POINTS IN LONG AND SHORT SUITS

Back in the days when hands were evaluated in terms of honor tricks, a singleton king wasn't assigned any value. This is silly—if partner has the ace, the singleton king will take a trick. Give partner the queen, and the singleton king will promote it. Even when the opponents have all the other high cards in the suit, a singleton king is likely to take a trick if it lies behind the ace—declarer probably will try a finesse.

A singleton ace always was given full value. However, although it was certain to take a trick, it wasn't doing its full quota of work—it promoted no other cards, and it had to be played the first time the suit was led.

Holdings such as Q-x and J-x-x aren't going to do you much good as declarer unless partner can help by producing other honors in the same suit. How do you allow for all this in counting points?

Again, you must try to use your judgment. Bear in mind that *the more low cards you and partner hold to back up your high cards, the more value your high cards assume.* Compare these two hands:

1. ♠ A 4 3   2. ♠ A 4 3
   ♡ A 4 3 2   ♡ K J 10 9
   ◇ A 3 2   ◇ A 3 2
   ♣ A 3 2   ♣ A 3 2

Both contain 16 high-card points, but the second hand has more potential. In hand 1 the aces have no lower cards to promote. In hand 2 the aces will buy declarer some time to establish his heart suit.

At the start of the bidding you should count one less distribution point for any honors unsupported by at least one lower card—thus, you count only 5 points for a singleton ace,

4 for a singleton king, etc. You don't count any distribution points for A K or any similar doubleton.

OTHER FACTORS IN HAND EVALUATION

The *location* of your high cards affects the value of your hand. You should open the bidding with

♠ A K 4 3 2   ♡ A 5 4 3 2   ◇ 3 2   ♣ 2

because you have 14 points, counting 3 for distribution. But you probably should pass with

♠ 6 5 4 3 2   ♡ 6 5 4 3 2   ◇ A K   ♣ A

because, although you have the same high-card strength, you have only 1 point in distribution. You tend to underbid a trifle when your high cards are concentrated in your short suits. You can overbid a trifle when the high cards lie in your long suits.

Honors in the same suit are worth more than honors in different suits. For instance:

♠ A Q 3 2   ♠ A 4 3 2
♡ 6 5   has more trick-taking power than   ♡ Q 5
◇ 7 6 5   ◇ K 6 5
♣ A K 3 2   ♣ A 4 3 2

Also,

♠ A K   ♠ A 2
♡ Q J 10 4 3   surely will produce more   ♡ Q 10 4 3 2
◇ 4 3 2   tricks than   ◇ J 4 3
♣ 4 3 2   ♣ K 4 3

especially if partner has no supporting cards in his hand.

Honors in suits your partner has bid invariably are worth more than other honors. If partner opens in hearts and rebids in diamonds, you would rather have

♠ A 7 6		♠ K Q 3
♡ Q J 4	than	♡ 5 4 3
◇ K 6 5		◇ J 4 3
♣ 6 5 4 2		♣ K J 3 2

even though both hands have 10 high-card points.

DECLARER'S ADVANTAGE

If you have 4-3-3-3 distribution, there is no reason for you to want to be declarer unless your side has the majority of the high cards—you may score some high-card tricks, but you have no long cards for your high cards to promote. What is more important, the enemy's high cards will score against you when you have a lot of possible losers.

However, give yourself a doubleton and you have a potential ruffing trick—you won't be able to ruff an ace or king, but you can ruff a queen. A singleton may be really worthwhile. If your partner has three or four small cards in that suit and you have plenty of trumps, your singleton will be worth a lot more than the 2 or 3 points you valued for it at the start—it will be worth two or three tricks.

If your partner has a singleton facing a suit in which you have several small cards, you have two well-fitting hands. If you also have lots of trumps, you don't need much in high cards to take a lot of tricks.

When each side has a good fit, experienced bidders are more likely to compete to a high level. They have much more to gain than to lose by getting to be declarer, and the side that finally buys the contract will often make it, helped by their fit.

The essence of successful competition is to find good fits and capitalize on them—but to do this you must take chances. This doesn't mean you should compete for the sheer joy of sticking our neck out. It means that, when you have good distribution, you should try to enter the auction some-how—the deal may belong to you.

Even if your side doesn't own the deal, there may be a cheap sacrifice available. You won't get rich sacrificing, but whenever you save a game at a cost of 300 points or less, you have cut your losses substantially.

Opening Bids

The opening bid is the cornerstone of both attack and defense. Experience has shown that the side that opens the bidding gains a great advantage, provided that responder (opener's partner) can count on opener for some definite minimum values.

TYPES OF OPENINGS

There are several types of opening bids. Some are used only with specific hands and are very descriptive. Others may be made with a wide variety of hands.

We will discuss no-trump openings first because they have standard meanings with little variation. We will follow with opening suit-bids of one, which are more complex and varied. (This is the workhorse bid in Jacoby and in all well-established systems. In our style this bid shows 11–22 high-card points.)

Next, we will take up more specialized suit-bids—the weak two-bid, the preemptive opening and the forcing two-club bid. Our two-club opening does not necessarily show clubs—it is an artificial bid denoting a strong two-bid in any of the four suits (or, on occasion, a very strong balanced hand). THIS TWO-CLUB BID IS OUR ONLY FORCING OPENING BID.

The following chart gives the high-card point requirements for various openings. The two most important things to remember are that (1) you can't afford not to open with 14 high-card points, and (2) your decision whether to open with 11 high-card points is based entirely on the look of your hand, not on your position at the table, the vulnerability, or the signs of the Zodiac.

HIGH-CARD POINTS	ACTION
0–4	Pass When you take any action you want your partner to know that you have some high cards
5–9	Open with a preemptive bid of three or four if your hand meets the requirements Otherwise pass
7–10	Open with a weak two-bid in spades hearts, or diamonds if your hand meets the requirements Otherwise pass
11	Open one of a good six-card or a very good five-card suit Otherwise pass
12–13	Opening one of a suit is permitted However, you may prefer to pass if you have 4-3-3-3 distribution or if most of your high-card strength consists of queens and jacks
14–15	Open one of a suit. With 14 HCP you have a full ace more than your share of the high cards. If you and partner both pass such a

hand, you would pass out a deal where a game contract might make easily

16–18	Open one no-trump if you meet the requirements Otherwise, open one of a suit or, rarely, a forcing two clubs.
19–20	Open one of a suit or, occasionally, a forcing two clubs.
21–22	Open two no-trump if you meet the requirements Otherwise, open a forcing two clubs or one of a suit
23 or more	Open three no-trump with 25–26 HCP if you meet the requirements Otherwise, open a forcing two clubs

Opening No-Trump Bids

All these bids give your partner a clear picture of your hand so he can direct the bidding from then on.

If your hand meets all the requirements for a no-trump opening, bid no-trump. If it doesn't, bid a suit. Bidding no-trump is a lot of fun, but if you use undisciplined no-trumps, you will make it impossible for your partner to take full advantage of these "picture bids."

These are the requirements for a no-trump opening.

1. Your high-card point count must be:

   16–18 .... to open one no-trump
   21–22 .... to open two no-trump
   25–26 .... to open three no-trump

2. Your distribution must be 5-3-3-2, 4-4-3-2, or 4-3-3-3. (In other words, you can have no singleton or void suit, and no more than one doubleton.)

In years past, it was a requirement that any doubleton had to contain one of the four top honors. Most modern experts are willing to open in no-trump with a worthless doubleton.

Note that, while the Jacoby one no-trump opening is identical to Standard American, the two no-trump and three no-trump openings have slightly narrower ranges. The gap between one no-trump and two no-trump is handled by a bidding sequence that starts with one of a suit, but this gap is one point narrower than in Standard American.

The 23–24 HCP no-trump hand, as well as no-trump hands with more than 26 HCP, will be covered when we come to the forcing two-club bid.

Opening One of a Suit

We have given you a definite rule about hands with 14 or more high-card points—they always are opened. We can give you equally definite rules about hands with 11–13 high-card points, but you may want to depart from them slightly if you are an experienced player.

With 11 HCP ... Pass most of the time. Open only when you have a suit of five or more cards headed by at least two of the top four honors, plus either a singleton or two doubletons.

With 12 HCP ... Don't open with 4-3-3-3 distribution. Pass occasionally with 4-4-3-2 distribution. Open with any other distribution.

With 13 HCP ... Open unless your distribution is 4-3-3-3 and your high-card strength is mostly in queens and jacks.

CHOOSING A SUIT TO OPEN

Once you decide to open the bidding, the next step is picking out a suit. There isn't much of a problem when you're lucky enough to hold at least one suit of five cards or more—just follow the standard rules:

1. With one suit of five cards or more, bid it.
2. With two suits of five cards or more, bid the longer one if the suits are unequal in length.* If the suits are the same length, bid the higher-ranking. Don't worry about the strength of the suit—any five-card suit is biddable.

MINIMUM BIDDABLE SUITS FOR OPENING

When you open one heart or one spade, you strongly suggest playing the hand in that suit. (True, you may wind up playing the hand in clubs or diamonds when you open one of those suits, but most of the time you will proceed to no-trump or a major suit—ten tricks are enough for a major suit game and nine will do for no-trump, but eleven tricks are needed for a game in a minor suit.) Therefore, when you open one heart or one spade, you prefer a longer or stronger suit.

A prevalent modern bidding style is to *promise* five or more cards for a major suit opening. However, Jacoby permits opening bids on certain four-card major suit holdings. While a five-card-major style may be slightly more accurate in constructive bidding, the ability to open on a good four-card major has compensating advantages—the opponents

---

*Many experts would treat a minimum hand with, say, five spades and six hearts as an exception. To prepare an economical rebid, they might open one spade on

♠ A K J 5 4   ♡ K 10 6 5 4 2   ◇ J 3   ♣ void

If partner responded one no-trump to a one-*heart* opening, a two-spade rebid by opener would be a *reverse* and would suggest more high-card strength. See pages 84 and 94.

can't enter the auction as easily over a major-suit opening, it seldom is necessary to open on a filthy minor suit, and major suit fits are lost less often.

In Jacoby, any five-card major or four-card minor is good enough to open. Four-card majors must be headed by five high-card points or three honors. Minimum holdings are A J 9 2 or Q J 10 2.

Here are some rules for choosing an opening bid when you lack a five-card suit. A study of these rules will show that, in fact, a four-card major is seldom opened.

—With just one biddable suit, open in it.
—With two biddable suits, open in the lower-ranking.
—With three biddable suits, open one diamond unless your singleton is in diamonds—in that case open one club.
—Certain three-card minor suits are considered biddable, as outlined under the next heading.

Opening one club with a three-card suit

While experts may disagree on the proper opening bid when you don't have a five-card suit or a good four-carder, everyone agrees that occasionally you must open with one club on only three cards. Here is an example:

♠ J 6 4 2   ♡ Q J 7   ◇ A 5 4   ♣ A Q 10

This hand contains 14 high-card points and must be opened. Opening one club is unpleasant, but any other opening is even more of a distortion. A one-club opening keeps the auction low and prepares an easy one-spade rebid if your partner responds in diamonds or hearts.

You don't plan to do much after this start except keep bidding as long as your partner forces you. You won't be happy if your partner raises to two clubs (as he may well do), but don't go into a state of shock—just pass and struggle with that contract. Two clubs may be makable, since partner is sure to have at least four-card club support for you.

Some players, especially those who use a five-card-major style, are likely to open one club on *any* three-card suit. Our style is not to open one club on a holding worse than Q-10-x—we like to have a couple of honors in case the opponents buy the contract and partner leads a club.

Do not leave this bid out of your repertory, but don't go to extremes and use it too often. It is a bid you must make when the alternative openings are worse; it is not a panacea for all your bidding problems.

Incidentally, we avoid opening one *diamond* on a three-card suit, but it may be the lesser evil with 4-4-3-2 distribution and poor major suits, or with 3-4-3-3 or 4-3-3-3 shape, terrible clubs and a poor major. Again, we prefer to have a couple of honors in the suit.

The subject of choosing a suit to open is very important, so we will give several examples.

♠ A Q 6 5   ♡ A J 3   ◇ J 4 3   ♣ Q 10 3

This is a mandatory opening, and both black suits are biddable. Open one club. Note that your rebid is easy—you can go to one spade if partner responds one diamond or one heart. You can raise a one-spade response to two spades, and you will pass if partner responds one no-trump or raises clubs.

Most hands with 4-3-3-3 or 3-4-3-3 distribution are opened with one club (or, occasionally, one diamond) in our style. But . . .

♠ A K J 3   ♡ A 6 5   ◇ J 5 4   ♣ J 5 4

Open one spade. You have robust spades, and no other suit is biddable.

♠ Q 6 5 3   ♡ A K 5   ◇ K Q 4   ♣ 9 6 3

Open one diamond.

41

With two four-card suits there are many possible combinations to consider.

♠ A Q 5 4   ♡ K 5 4 3   ◇ 4 3   ♣ A J 3

Open one club.

♠ K J 10 5   ♡ A Q 9 3   ◇ A 4   ♣ 10 7 6

Both major suits are biddable. Open one heart, the lower-ranking.

♠ A Q 10 6   ♡ Q 7 6 5   ◇ 6 4 2   ♣ A Q

This is one of the few times we open with a four-card spade suit.

♠ A J 10 6   ♡ A K 6   ◇ J 6 5 2   ♣ 3 2

Open one diamond.

♠ A Q 5 2   ♡ 7 6   ◇ A 4 3   ♣ K J 7 6
♠ 7 6   ♡ A Q 5 2   ◇ A 4 3   ♣ K J 7 6

In both cases open one club.

♠ 7 6   ♡ A Q 5 4   ◇ A J 7 6   ♣ K 3 2

Open one diamond.

♠ 6 5   ♡ A 4 3   ◇ A J 6 5   ♣ K Q 4 3

Open one club.

♠ 2   ♡ A 6 5 4   ◇ A J 5 4   ♣ K Q 3 2
♠ A 6 5 4   ♡ 2   ◇ A J 5 4   ♣ K Q 3 2

In both cases open one diamond.

♠ K J 6 5 ♡ A J 6 5 ◇ 4 ♣ K Q 5 4

Open one club.

NO BIDDABLE SUITS

We freely admit that there are some hands which, though they must be opened, have *no* biddable suits.

♠ K 7 6 5 ♡ K 6 5 4 ◇ J 4 3 ♣ A K

Open one diamond.

♠ K 6 5 4 ♡ K 6 5 4 ◇ A K ♣ J 6 5

Open one club.

Both these hands have too much in high cards to pass. In each case we have manufactured an opening by choosing a suit that is nearly biddable. Our solution isn't perfect, but very little in this world is.

Opening Weak Two-Bids

There must be experts somewhere who still cling to the old-fashioned strong two-bids, but all the experts we know have found that a forcing two-club opening on *all* very strong hands works quite well.

This releases opening bids of two spades, two hearts, and two diamonds for other purposes. There are many possible ways to employ these bids, but most experts use them to show hands just below opening-bid strength with a good six-card suit.

You can make weak two-bids complicated if you like, but Jacoby restricts them to hands with specifically 7–10 high-card points, a six-card suit headed by at least two of the top four honors, and 6-3-3-1 or 6-3-2-2 distribution. This makes them real "picture bids" and allows your partner to judge the subsequent bidding accurately.

Here are some typical weak two-bids:

♠ A K Q 10 6 4	♠ A 8 4	♠ 9
♡ 6 5	♡ K Q 10 9 8 4	♡ K 7 6
◇ 8 4 3	◇ 6 4 3	◇ A J 10 8 5 4
♣ 7 2	♣ 8	♣ 9 8 2
Open two spades.	Open two hearts.	Open two diamonds.

When you open these hands with a weak two-bid, you do not know what your partner and the opponents hold. Perhaps your partner has a good hand—in that case he can decide what to do. Unless he has a fit for your suit, he probably will just pass even if he has a good hand.

Suppose that the opponents hold most of the power. Your weak two-bid may not keep them out of the bidding, but you will jam up their start. They must start bidding at the two- or three-level, and they will have a lot more trouble finding their best contract than if they had been left to bid with no interference.

You seldom will be hurt when you make one of these weak openings. You occasionally will find yourself the victim of a penalty double, but no bid in bridge is absolutely loss-proof. On the other hand, if you pass with one of these hands and try to back in later, you are much more likely to get into trouble. And if you never bid at all, you are letting your opponents dominate the bidding.

Preemptive Openings

A preemptive opening is a bid of three or four in a suit (or, rarely, five of a minor suit). It is intended to keep the opponents out of the bidding entirely or, failing that, to crowd their bidding so they won't find their best contract.

With a good hand don't preempt—start with a one-bid. The deal may well belong to your side, and you want plenty of room to exchange information.

There are two requirements for a preemptive opening:

1. You should have 5–9 or occasionally 10 high-card points.
2. You should have a strong seven-card suit at the three-level; a strong eight-card suit at the four-level.

Are you likely to be doubled for penalty when you preempt? Yes, you are, so you don't want to risk a loss of more than 500 points—down three tricks not vulnerable or down two tricks vulnerable. Therefore, when you preempt take note of the sure winners your long suit will produce. You may count a holding like

KQJ8654

as six tricks. Of course, it is safer to have

KQJ10987

The opening bid of four of a major is a special case. You are very likely to be doubled at these contracts, so it is advisable to have something in reserve in the way of distribution.

♠ A K Q J 8 7 6   ♥ 2   ♦ 2   ♣ J 1 0 7 5

is worth a four-spade opening even if you are vulnerable. If partner has the king of clubs and nothing else, you just might bring the game home. But

♠ A K Q J 8 7 6   ♥ 3 2   ♦ 5 4   ♣ 3 2

is a poor four-spade opening at any vulnerability. You may suffer a substantial loss when a profit was possible.

Naturally, suits that contain more than seven cards are even more tempting for a preemptive opening bid. However, if you have a nine- or ten-card suit with good controls on the side (so that slam is a possibility), don't preempt. You may discourage your partner from responding, stalling your side at a part-score or game contract.

The Forcing Two-Club Opening

The standard strong two-bid was a great thing back in 1929 when it was invented jointly by Oswald Jacoby, Theodore Lightner and Waldemar von Zedtwitz. Then, in the forties, experts began to realize that a two-club opening could get the job done, and at the same time release the bids of two spades, two hearts, and two diamonds to show other kinds of hands.

We can assure you that the forcing two-club opening is effective and very easy to learn. Though almost all experts use it, it is one bid that is well within the reach of bridge players at all levels.

When we put the forcing two-club bid into Jacoby, we decided on a set of new and simple responses. We have found that these simplified responses help our own bidding tremendously. We'll get around to them later.

RULES FOR THE TWO-CLUB OPENING

A forcing two-club opening is a catchall strong bid. It is made on a balanced hand with either 23–24 high-card points or 27 high-card points or more. (If you have 26 high-card points and a balanced hand, you open three no-trump.)

It also is made with any hand on which you would have opened a strong two-bid in a suit. We can't give exact point-count requirements here, but we consider 16 HCP as the minimum. Any forcing two-club opening suggests good defensive values (at least four sure defensive tricks), and this requirement is hard to satisfy with borderline high-card strength. However, if you go down to 15 high-card points once a year, you won't be committing a bridge felony.

Another test for opening two clubs with the 16–22 high-card-point hands is playing strength. If the playing tricks in your own hand add up to within one trick of game, you have enough playing strength to open two clubs. Suppose you pick up

♠ AKQ1065 ♡ AK93 ◇ A8 ♣ 3

You expect to take five or six tricks in spades (call it five and a half), two or three in hearts (say, two and a half), and one in diamonds. By conservative estimate you can take nine tricks with spades as trumps. Since you also have plenty of defensive values, you may open two clubs.

♠ AJ54 ♡ AQ65 ◇ A ♣ AQ32

This hand has more high-card points than the one above, but you must open it with one club and hope partner can respond. You lack the certain playing tricks to force to game.

RESPONDING TO THE TWO-CLUB OPENING

There are almost as many methods to respond to two clubs as there are experts, but Jacoby has developed a new one. After trying it with hundreds of computer-dealt hands, we found that it is both the simplest and most effective method.

The negative response is two diamonds, and it shows a real bust: 0–3 high-card points. After this response, the auction is forcing only to two no-trump, three of a major, or once in a blue moon, four of a minor. After any other response, the auction is forcing to game (unless the opponents start bidding and you decide to stop off and double them for penalty).

Each response artificially shows high-card points, as follows:

Two diamonds .... 0–3 high-card points
Two hearts .... 4–6 high-card points
Two spades ...... 7–9 high-card points
Two no-trump .... 10 or more high-card points

REBIDDING AFTER THE TWO-CLUB OPENING

You will know a lot about your partner's hand right away, since the response will have told you his high-card point count. In general you want to tell partner about what sort of two-club opening you hold.

With a strong two-bid in a suit	bid your suit.
With 23–24 HCP, balanced	make a minimum rebid in no-trump.
With 27–28 HCP, balanced	make a single jump in no-trump.
With 29 or more HCP, balanced	let your conscience be your guide.

From here the auction should develop easily, but responder has a couple of special bids available if opener shows a strong two-bid in a suit. Responder can jump straight to game with a poor hand but excellent trump support. He also can raise just one level with trump support in addition to high-card strength. Responder's bid of a new suit should show a suit at least as good as Q J 10 xx; with a long, weak suit he should prefer some other bid.

OPENER   RESPONDER
2 ♣   2 ◇
2 ♡   ?

♠ 76   ♡ K 1065   ◇ 65   ♣ 97542

Bid four hearts. You have good support but nothing else.

OPENER   RESPONDER
2 ♣   2 ♡
2 ♠   ?

♠ K64   ♡ K654   ◇ 8765   ♣ 43

Bid three spades. A raise to four spades would deny as much as a king outside trumps.

OPENER   RESPONDER
2 ♣   2 ♠
3 ♣   ?

♠ K43   ♡ J7653   ◇ A103   ♣ 43

Bid three no-trump. Do not bid three hearts on such a ragged suit.

For more on the development of the auction after a two-club opening, see the discussion of slam bidding, pages 118–29.

Responding to No-Trump Openings

RAISES

Your partner's no-trump opening shows balanced distribution. If you have balanced distribution also, your responses are just a matter of adding your own points to the points your partner's no-trump opening showed. A one no-trump opening shows 16–18. If you have 7 points or less, your total will be less than 26. You therefore don't want to be in game. If you are satisfied to play in no-trump, you pass.

Suppose you have 8 or 9 points. Opposite a 16-point no-trump the total is 24 or 25—again you do not want to be in game. But opposite an 18-point hand the total is 26 or 27—game should be a good shot.

How do you handle this? Just raise to two no-trump with balanced hands of 8–9 points. Partner will pass with 16 and go to game with 18. With 17 he will use his judgment, looking at his tens and nines.

With 10–14 high-card points you want to be in game—$10 + 16 = 26$. You don't want to be in slam—$18 + 14 =$ only 32

With 15–16 you invite slam with four no-trump. This four no-trump bid is not Blackwood—it's just a no-trump raise.

With better hands you can either bid six no-trump or seven no-trump directly, depending on your point count. Or you can try for a grand slam by responding with five no-trump—

this forces partner to bid at least six no-trump and invites him to bid seven.

All this is simple indeed. Nevertheless, there is one artificial gadget you may need when you have a balanced hand opposite a no-trump opening. Suppose you hold

♠ A Q 6 5   ♡ 7 2   ♦ K 9 4   ♣ Q 7 6 2

You have 11 high-card points, so three no-trump may be a reasonable contract. However, if your partner holds four cards in spades, it's very likely that four spades will be even better. You can get there if you use the Jacoby version of the Stayman convention.

THE STAYMAN CONVENTION

Every expert uses some form of this convention to find 4-4 major suit fits and for other valuable purposes. It's a simple gadget that every bridge player can use. Here is the Jacoby form of Stayman:

A two-club response to one no-trump is artificial and a one-round force. Partner must rebid two spades if he has four cards in spades, two hearts with four hearts and two diamonds without four cards in either major. These are the no-trump opener's only permissible rebids. (With four cards in *both* majors, most experts show the spades first.)

In the Jacoby version of Stayman you don't need a good hand to use this artificial two-club bid. Suppose you hold

♠ Q 10 9 6 5   ♡ J 8 7 2   ♦ 5 4   ♣ 8 3

If partner opens one no-trump, you don't want him to play it there because your hand is not balanced. You respond two clubs, and if he rebids two spades or two hearts, you are happy to pass. If he rebids two diamonds, you proceed to two spades. He is supposed to pass that.

Be sure your partner knows you are using this variation of Stayman. Some people play that the use of Stayman always implies interest in game, and you can't afford to have partner bid on over two spades when you have a hand this weak.

INVITING GAME AFTER A TWO-CLUB RESPONSE

If partner's rebid is in your four-card major suit, you raise to three as a game invitation with 8 or 9 points. If he responds two diamonds or bids the major you don't have, you bid two no-trump, inviting him to go on to three no-trump. Here is an example:

♠ K976   ♡ 32   ◇ A1054   ♣ J97

You have 8 high-card points, plus a ten and two nines. Partner opens one no-trump and you respond two clubs. If partner rebids two hearts or two diamonds, you bid two no-trump. He will pass with 16, bid game with 18, and use his judgment with 17. If your partner's rebid is two spades, you raise to three spades. Again, you are leaving the final decision to him.

What do you do with 5-4 in the majors and a good hand such as

♠ Q10965   ♡ K974   ◇ A2   ♣ J8

You still respond two clubs. If partner bids either major, you take him to game there. If he bids two diamonds, you jump to three spades—this is forcing and asks him to choose between three no-trump and four spades.

OTHER RESPONSES TO ONE NO-TRUMP

What do you do when you have a bad hand with a long suit, and you want to play below game in your suit?

Bid your suit at the two-level. Responses of two in any suit *except clubs* show weak hands, such as

♠ KJ7654   ♡ 632   ◇ 54   ♣ 82

Respond two spades with this hand. Partner is expected to let you play it there.

What do you do when you want to play a part-score in clubs?
You cannot sign off at two clubs, but there are ways of stopping at *three* clubs. Some players respond two clubs, then bid three clubs over opener's rebid to sign off. There also is a method to stop low in clubs using the Jacoby transfer bid (page 58). If you prefer to avoid complexities, you can just pass one no-trump with a club suit and run only if your partner gets doubled.

What do jumps to three of a suit mean?
They are forcing and strong, especially in a minor suit, and ask opener to show support if he has it. They range from a hand with mild slam interest to a definite slam hand. Respond three spades on

♠ K Q 7 5 3   ♡ 6 5   ◇ A 7 6   ♣ A J 2

If opener raises, try for slam. If opener returns to three no-trump, denying three-card support for spades, prefer a conservative pass.

What do jumps to four of a suit mean?
In a major suit they show a hand like

♠ 2   ♡ A Q 9 7 5 4 3   ◇ J 1 0 3   ♣ 8 2

You want to play in four hearts and have no interest in slam.
You never respond at the four-level in a minor suit as a natural bid, but some players use a four-club response as an ace-asking bid (the Gerber convention—see page 123).

In summary:

Two spades, two hearts, ... and two diamonds	Weakness bids that show no interest in game and require partner to pass.
Three clubs and three . . . . . . diamonds	Strong one-suited hands with definite slam interest. With a good club or diamond hand but without slam interest you just bid three no-trump.
Three hearts and three . . . . . spades	Strong one-suited hands with slam interest.
Four hearts and four . . . . spades	Sign-offs. You want to be in game but have no slam interest.

How do you look for a 4-4 major suit fit if your partner's one-no-trump opening is overcalled?

It's better to use a three-club bid to show clubs, so you must cue-bid the opponent's suit. Suppose partner opens one no-trump and the next hand overcalls two hearts. You bid three hearts, Stayman, with

♠ A Q 5 4   ♡ 6 5   ◇ K 10 5 4   ♣ Q 4 3

Can you use both Stayman and the Jacoby transfer bid?

You certainly can—they complement each other perfectly.

After you have learned Stayman thoroughly, we suggest you go on to the chapter on the Jacoby transfer and add it to your repertory.

RESPONDING TO A TWO-NO-TRUMP OPENING

Raises on balanced hands are really easy. Your partner has shown 21–22 high-card points. With 0–3, the maximum total is 25—you pass. With 4–10, the minimum total is 25, the maximum 32—you bid three no-trump. You bid four no-trump with 11 or a bad-looking 12—this is a raise, not Blackwood. With better hands, you bid a slam or invite a grand slam by bidding five no-trump, depending on your exact point count.

The only way to stop short of game when your partner opens two no-trump is to pass. You may bid a five-card suit or longer, seeking support in partner's hand, but the auction is forcing to game.

Can you see Stayman after a two-no-trump opening?

Yes. You still may want to look for a 4-4 major suit fit. Of course, you must be prepared to play in game if you use Stayman here.

RESPONDING TO A THREE-NO-TRUMP OPENING

You don't find yourself facing too many three-no-trump openings. Raise in accordance with your high cards—four no-trump is a slam-invitational raise. Bid four of a major suit if you want to play it there. Many partnerships agree in advance to use a four-club response as ace-asking and a four-diamond response as Stayman.

The Jacoby Transfer Bid

The Jacoby transfer bid allows the opening no-trump bidder, whose hand is strong, to become declarer, even though his partner has a long suit. Oswald and James Jacoby did not really invent this bid, but we did formalize it and make it practical. You can get full value from your no-trump openings if you add the Jacoby transfer bid (often referred to as JTB) to your use of the Stayman convention. Here is how JTB is used.

Responses of two diamonds and two hearts to a one-no-trump opening are artificial—opener is asked to "transfer" by bidding the next higher suit. The two-diamond response says to partner: "I have at least five hearts. Bid two hearts and I will tell you more about my hand." The two-heart response carries a similar message, except that it shows at least five spades.

Let's look at two examples of JTB at work. Partner opens one no-trump, and you hold:

1. ♠ KJ7654   ♡ 632   ◇ 54   ♣ 82
2. ♠ KJ7654   ♡ A32   ◇ 54   ♣ 82

Using standard methods, you would bid two spades with hand #1 and hope to play it there. With hand #2 you would respond four spades and expect to make that contract.

If you are using JTB, you respond two *hearts* with both hands. Partner dutifully rebids two spades. With the first hand you pass; with the second you bid four spades.

It has taken a little longer to reach the same contracts, but you enjoy an appreciable advantage if you have used the JTB. Your partner, holding the stronger hand, is now declarer—the opening lead will come up to his hand. That is much better than having partner put down his hand as the dummy and watching an attacking lead made through his high-card combinations. We average a gain of half a trick per deal by having the weaker hand be dummy. We make many contracts that other pairs would not make, and we also make a lot more overtricks.

There is another advantage for hands such as #1. When you respond two spades using standard methods, you expect your partner to pass. But sometimes your partner has a maximum no-trump opening, perhaps with good spade support, and he decides to raise you—he is afraid you might have close to an invitational hand. Or perhaps your partner simply forgets that you have made a weakness bid, and he bids again. When you use JTB, partner is compelled to bid two spades himself. He may be sorry to hear you pass, but he will smile when he sees that your dummy has very few high cards.

HOW TO TRANSFER TO A MINOR SUIT IN JTB

With a good minor suit hand you need not transfer—the advantage of having the opening lead come up to the strong hand is reduced. But with a bad hand and a long minor you either forget about bidding entirely or you put JTB's two-spade response to work.

The two-spade response shows a hand like one of these:

♠ 543   ♡ 3   ◊ 864   ♣ QJ9765
♠ 543   ♡ 3   ◊ QJ9765   ♣ 864

The opening no-trump bidder must reply three clubs. If responder has a long club suit and a bad hand, he passes—the three-club contract is played from opener's side. If responder has a diamond bust, he goes to three diamonds. He hasn't allowed opener to become declarer in diamonds, but he has reached a better contract than one no-trump.

QUESTIONS AND ANSWERS ABOUT JTB

How do you rebid after making a Jacoby transfer?

As the above examples show, you can pass or bid game in your suit. You also can bid three no-trump, which gives partner a choice of contracts. Here is a typical hand with which you would transfer to hearts and then bid three no-trump:

♠ K4 ♡ Q9764 ◇ J54 ♣ A96

With 10 HCP, no singleton, and honors in all suits, you first bid two diamonds as a transfer. Then you follow with three no-trump to suggest that you would be happy to play that game contract. Your partner would certainly bid four hearts if he had four cards in the suit, and he'd often correct to four hearts with only a three-card heart holding.

Here's another hand:

♠ J4 ♡ Q9764 ◇ J54 ♣ A96

With 8 HCP and a five-card suit you are interested in game. Transfer with two diamonds and continue with two no-trump. Partner can pass or bid three no-trump, three hearts, or four hearts—his action will depend on how strong his no-trump opening is and how good his hearts are.

Another hand:

♠ KJ7654 ♡ Q102 ◇ 54 ♣ 32

This is an impossible hand to describe accurately unless you use JTB. First you transfer with two hearts, and then you raise to three spades, inviting game.

What about two-suited hands?
Look at this one:

♠ 3   ♡ A Q 7 6 5   ◇ K J 9 6 4   ♣ 10 3

You want to be in game opposite a one no-trump opening.
Transfer with two diamonds, and then bid three diamonds to
show your second suit. This bid in a new suit is a game force.
It gives partner a chance to show a preference for hearts,
diamonds or no-trump. It may even lead to a slam if partner
holds an ideal hand, like this one:

♠ A 10 8   ♡ K 3   ◇ A Q 8 7   ♣ A 7 6 2

Suppose opener has

♠ K Q J 5   ♡ J 8   ◇ Q 10 4   ♣ A K 8 6

Over three diamonds opener will bid three no-trump, and you
will be in the right contract.

**What happens if your partner opens one no-trump and the
next hand overcalls or doubles?**
Forget about JTB and just play standard methods.

Should you use JTB after a one-no-trump overcall?
No. You don't mind being declarer, since most of the
adverse strength will be to your left.

**What about using JTB in responding to a two-no-trump
opening?**
You can and should do so. JTB is especially effective here
because it is even more important for the strong hand to be
declarer.

Do you ever jump in response to a transfer bid?
Yes, but not often. If your opening no-trump is maximum
and you have four cards in partner's suit, you can jump to

three of his suit to show this type of hand. Here is an example:

♠ KJ87　♡ A2　◇ A976　♣ AQ9

Jump to three spades if your partner makes a JTB of two hearts in response to your opening no-trump.

You also can jump after a transfer response to a two-no-trump opening.

♠ K4　♡ KQ98　◇ AK7　♣ AK104

Bid four hearts after partner's three-diamond JTB. You will have a play for four hearts if partner has no more than five hearts to the jack. If he has as much as six little hearts, you will be a favorite to make game.

Responding to Opening Bids of One of a Suit

Our responses to one of a suit are standard, with one exception—we use the *limit* single-jump raise, showing 10–12 points, instead of the forcing single-jump raise, which shows 13–15 points. You don't have to adopt these limit jump raises, but we are sure that once you try them, you'll never go back to the forcing variety.

Limit raises are used by most of today's experts. They fill the gap between the single raise (7–9 points) and the forcing jump raise, and they simplify your bidding in still another way. In Standard American many jump raises are nonforcing—for instance, the jump raise of opener's second suit, the jump raise of an overcall, and the jump raise by a passed hand all are generally played as nonforcing. In Jacoby, *all* jump raises, while they may be strongly invitational, become nonforcing. However, when your partner gives you a jump raise, bear in mind that he will like it if you go on to game. Respect his wishes with any excuse.

In Jacoby a response of two in a lower-ranking suit (for example, a two-club response to one spade) shows at least 11 points, including 9 points or more in high cards. This is in accordance with today's standard expert practice.

THE PASS AS A RESPONSE

An opening one-bid shows a 13-point minimum hand and an indefinite maximum, but the great majority of these openings are made with fewer than 20 high-card points. Therefore, if your hand is worth 5 points or less, there is little chance that the combined hands will contain 26 points, the number necessary for a probable game in a major suit or in no-trump. You should pass. There is no advantage in bidding when you have nothing to justify the action.

WHEN TO RESPOND

You should *not* pass with 6 points or more, since you are likely to miss a game if your partner holds as much as 20— $20 + 6 = 26$.

Furthermore, $13 + 7 = 20$. Even if your partner has a minimum opening, you should be safe at one no-trump or, if you can locate a trump fit, at two of a suit.

TYPES OF RESPONSES

There are three types of responses—raises, new-suit bids, and responses in no-trump.

Always raise your partner in a major suit if you can. You should prefer to play in a major suit contract when you and your partner have enough trumps.

If your partner opens with a minor suit, you should prefer to respond in a major suit rather than raise the minor—it pays to look for a possible major suit fit. Consequently, an immediate raise in a minor suit tends to deny any four-card or longer major suit holding, as well as the requirements for a response in no-trump.

Raises and no-trump responses all are "picture bids"— they show responder's point count right away. New-suit bids cover a wide range of high-card strength and distributions. As such, they are exploratory in nature.

RAISES

The first requirement for a raise is adequate trump support. For a single raise of a major suit, three-card support is sufficient. For all other raises you need at least four-card support.

The advantage in having four or more cards in support of partner's suit is substantial. When you hold this number, you should add *support points* to the high-card and distributional points you already counted.

Add 1 extra point for each trump you hold more than three.
Add 1 extra point for each singleton or void.

The point-count requirements for a raise:

Single raise	6–9 points, including at least 3 high-card points
Single-jump raise	10–12 points, including at least 7 high-card points
Double-jump raise	13 or more points, but no more than 10 high-card points

Note that the table above doesn't cover all possible hands with support for partner's suit. For example, you often will have enough strength for a jump raise, but only three trumps. With such hands *temporize* by responding in a new suit, and show your trump support by raising later. With 13 or more points including more than 10 high-card points, you also respond in a new suit and raise your partner to game or higher later. (Also, see the Jacoby two-no-trump response, page 130.)

In the following examples partner opens one heart.

♠ A Q 4 3   ♡ Q 8 7   ◊ 5 4 3   ♣ 7 6 2

Raise to two hearts. Do not complicate matters by showing the spades when there is a known fit in hearts.

♠ 76   ♡ KQ54   ♢ AJ76   ♣ 654

Raise to three hearts.

♠ void   ♡ K6542   ♢ A7653   ♣ 765

Raise to four hearts. The double-jump raise is a two-edged sword. Perhaps you will make four hearts. If not, you will have made it difficult for the opponents to bid spades, where *they* may have a game.

♠ K943   ♡ Q76   ♢ AQ2   ♣ 765

Respond one spade. You will show heart support later, but no *immediate* heart raise is appropriate.

RESPONSES IN A NEW SUIT

A new-suit response by an unpassed hand is forcing for one round. In theory any suit of four or more cards is biddable, although you naturally would rather not bid a worthless four-card suit. The point-count limits are:

At the one-level	7–17 points, including at least 3 high-card points
At the two-level in ..... a lower-ranking suit	11–17 points, including at least 9 high-card points
With a single jump	18 or more points, including at least 13 high-card points

In the following examples partner opens one heart.

♠ K J 3 2   ♡ 8 4   ◇ 9 6 5   ♣ K 7 3 2

Respond one spade. You have 7 points in high cards and a satisfactory spade suit.

♠ K 8 6 5   ♡ 6 5   ◇ A J 7 6 5   ♣ 5 4

Respond one spade. You lack the high-card strength to show the diamonds.

♠ A Q J 4   ♡ 8 4   ◇ K Q 7 6 5   ♣ Q 3

You have enough to respond two diamonds. A one-spade response is possible, but you have 14 points in high cards. With such a good hand you can afford to show your longest suit first, planning to bid the spades next.

In the following examples partner opens one club.

♠ K J 3 2   ♡ 8 4   ◇ K 1 0 7 6   ♣ 8 5 4

Respond one diamond. This hand also qualifies for a one-spade response, but with two four-card suits we prefer to show the lower one first.

♠ Q J 4 3 2   ♡ 8 4   ◇ A J 9 7 6   ♣ 5

Respond one spade. This time you have two five-card suits, so you respond in the higher-ranking.

♠ 5 4   ♡ K Q 6 5   ◇ A 4   ♣ Q 7 5 4 2

Respond one heart. Look for a major-suit fit before raising clubs.

RESPONDING IN NO-TRUMP

When you can't raise your partner directly or bid a suit of your own at the one-level, you respond one no-trump with 6–9 high-card points. (You occasionally may have to make this response with unbalanced distribution.)

Other no-trump responses show balanced distribution as well as stoppers in all unbid suits. A jump to two no-trump shows 13–15 high-card points. A jump to three no-trump shows 16–18 high-card points.

In the following examples partner opens one heart.

♠ Q J 4   ♡ 8 4   ◇ K J 8 4 3   ♣ 7 5 4

Respond one no-trump. You hold 7 high-card points, enough for a response at the one level but not for a two-diamond bid.

♠ K J 3   ♡ 4   ◇ K J 8 4 3   ♣ 7 5 4 2

Respond one no-trump even though your pattern is unbalanced. You must do something, but you still don't have enough to bid a new suit at the two-level.

♠ K 6 5 4   ♡ 4 3   ◇ K Q 5 4 3   ♣ J 3

Respond one spade. Look for a possible spade fit.

♠ K 6 5   ♡ J 5 4   ◇ A Q 7 6   ♣ A 1 0 4

Respond two no-trump. This is forcing to game.

♠ K 6 5   ♡ K 6 5   ◇ A Q 7 6   ♣ A J 3

Respond three no-trump. When you make this response, you are using up a lot of your own bidding room. Therefore, you prefer to have the ideal pattern—4-3-3-3—so partner will have some idea whether to bid again if he has an unbalanced hand. A three no-trump response is *not* forcing because you have arrived in game.

♠ K65   ♡ A65   ◇ 543   ♣ AQ76

Respond two clubs. With nothing in diamonds you may not respond two no-trump.

♠ K6   ♡ A7   ◇ Q643   ♣ AJ654

Respond two clubs. Your hand isn't balanced, so you can't jump to two no-trump.

JUMP SHIFTS

Once in a while, your hand will be so good that you'll know immediately you want to bid a slam or at least invite one. When you hold 18 or more points with at least 13 in high cards, you may show your great strength right away with a jump shift. A jump shift is a single jump in a new suit—for instance, three hearts over one spade, or two hearts over one diamond. This bid is forcing to game and invites slam.

The ideal time to jump-shift is when you know *where* the contract is likely to be played—in your suit, your partner's suit, or in no-trump.

In the following examples partner opens one diamond.

♠ AKQ10765   ♡ K5   ◇ 83   ♣ A6

Jump to two spades. You have 16 high-card points plus a self-sufficient suit. You will rebid spades at your next turn, telling partner that you have a strong hand with a very good suit of your own.

♠ AQJ93   ♡ 32   ◇ K1065   ♣ AK

Jump to two spades. You have 17 high-card points plus 1 for the doubleton. At your next turn you intend to support partner's diamonds.

♠ A Q 8 5 3   ♡ A Q 4   ◇ Q 5   ♣ K J 10

Jump to two spades, planning to bid three no-trump next. You tell partner that you are interested in slam, and you have a good spade suit located in a strong balanced hand.

♠ A Q J 3   ♡ A J 5 4   ◇ 7   ♣ A K 4 3

Respond one heart. You are unsure what suit will be best for trumps, so save room to look for a suit by staying low. If you find a fit, you can bid strongly.

SUMMARY OF RESPONSES

You raise to show support for partner's suit, bid a new suit to explore for a fit, and bid no-trump to show a good balanced hand or a weak one (balanced or unbalanced) that qualifies for no other response. Your possible calls with respect to your point count are reviewed below:

With 0–5 points	Pass. There is no point in attacking without ammunition.
With 6–7 points	Respond one no-trump or one of a suit, or give a single raise with support. Plan to stop bidding at the first opportunity.
With 8–9 points	Bid as though you had 6–7 points, except that if partner invites you to bid again, you will do so.

With 10–12 points . . . . .   Do not insist on game but plan to invite. Do not respond one no-trump or give a single raise.

With 13–17 points . . . . .   Make sure that game is reached.

With 18 points . . . .   Try for a slam, often with an immediate jump shift. With as many as 20 points insist on slam.

USING YOUR JUDGMENT

A good player isn't afraid to use his judgment in making bidding decisions. You will learn from experience when a hand is worth a little more or less than its point count actually indicates. You also should learn to modify your responses slightly to allow for this.

If you feel like responding with 6 bad high-card points or even with 5 high-card points that include an ace, do so. Some very weak hands almost cry out for action. If you feel like passing with 7 points, try to resist the urge. Remember, $7 + 19 = 26$.

One-no-trump responses and single raises are limited to a maximum of 9 points, but we occasionally choose one of these responses with a poor 10.

Some 12-point hands look mighty good—if your partner opens the bidding, don't be afraid to insist on game with them. Some 13-point supporting hands don't look as good as they might—just give a limit single-jump raise in such cases.

In the following examples partner opens one spade.

♠ 3   ♡ A J 8 6 4   ◊ 1 0 6 5 4 2   ♣ J 5

Respond one no-trump. Game in hearts could be makable if partner rebids in hearts and has a little extra strength.

♠ 103 ♡ KJ104 ◇ 10965 ♣ Q98

Respond one no-trump. You have plenty of tens and nines.

♠ 86 ♡ QJ5 ◇ KJ65 ♣ QJ52

Just respond one no-trump despite the 10 high-card points. When you have this many queens and jacks, you aren't going anywhere unless partner has a very strong hand.

♠ 1084 ♡ A104 ◇ A97 ♣ A1094

Respond two no-trump. This hand is likely to make game opposite any minimum.

♠ Q854 ♡ J6 ◇ KQ9 ♣ K754

Just respond three spades. You have to scrape the bottom of the barrel to find 13 supporting points. If your partner doesn't go on, you're not likely to be missing a game.

As a last word, let us remind you that you should deduct 1 point for 4-3-3-3 distribution when raising your partner.

Responding to a Weak Two-Bid

When you open a weak two-bid, you have given partner a pretty good picture of your hand—you have a six-card suit with 7–10 high-card points. Unless partner has the equivalent of a sound opening bid or better, he doesn't have to worry about your side having a game.

However, he may worry about a game in the other direction. In that case he may want to raise you in an attempt to keep the opponents out of the bidding. He also may want to bid a suit of his own that he thinks is better than yours. He can't do either one if you are going to take his raise or new-suit bid seriously. But if your side is playing Jacoby, you will not go crazy merely because partner responded to your weak two-bid.

If partner does have enough to think of game or slam opposite your weak two-bid, there is one forcing response he can make—two no-trump. This says: "Tell me more about your hand!"

Do you have a solid suit? In that case rebid three no-trump. Do you have 9–10 high-card points? Rebid three of another suit in which you hold an ace or a king. Do you have 7–8 high-card points? Then just return to three of your suit.

We repeat the examples given on page 44.

73

1. ♠ A K Q 10 6 4	2. ♠ A 8 4	3 ♠ 9
♡ 6 5	♡ K Q 10 9 8 4	♡ K 7 6
◇ 8 4 3	◇ 6 4 3	◇ A J 10 8 5 4
♣ 7 2	♣ 8	♣ 9 8 2
Open two	Open two	Open two
spades.	hearts.	diamonds.

With example 1 if partner responds two no-trump, rebid three no-trump—you have a solid suit. With example 2 rebid three spades—with 9 high-card points you may show a side ace or king. With example 3 rebid three diamonds—you have only 8 high-card points.

The response of two of a higher-ranking suit is not forcing, but opener is invited to raise to three with a reasonable weak two-bid and support for responder's suit. Thus, if you open two hearts with example 2 and partner responds with two spades, you should raise to three spades. AVOID REBID-DING YOUR OWN SUIT IF PARTNER BIDS A NEW SUIT IN RESPONSE TO YOUR WEAK TWO-BID.

Nonjump bids in a new suit at the three-level also are played as invitational. *Jumps* in a new suit below game are very strong invitations but may be passed. All game bids and single raises are sign-offs.

Here are some examples of responding to a weak two-heart opening.

♠ K J 9 7   ♡ 2   ◇ A Q 8 4   ♣ J 10 9 5

Pass. Don't try for game. Let your partner struggle with a two-heart contract unless the opponents are kind enough to compete.

♠ K 3   ♡ 2   ◇ A 9 7 6 5   ♣ K J 9 4 3

Pass. Don't try to find a minor suit fit.

♠ A Q J 8 7 6   ♡ 2   ◊ 9 5 4   ♣ 1 0 6 2

Bid two spades. You expect to take as many tricks in spades as in hearts, and you have indicated a good lead if fourth hand competes.

♠ A Q J 8 7 6 5   ♡ 2   ◊ A 4   ♣ J 1 0 3

Bid three spades. You want to invite game, but you aren't strong enough to force.

♠ A Q J 9 4   ♡ 2   ◊ A K 7 5   ♣ A J 4

Bid two no-trump. There may even be a slam if partner can show a spade feature (which must be the king) in reply to your force. You will make sure that game is reached.

♠ K J 9 7   ♡ 2   ◊ A Q 9   ♣ K Q J 9 8

Bid three no-trump. You are gambling, but it is the sort of gamble that is likely to pay off.

♠ K Q 2   ♡ J 7   ◊ A K 5 4   ♣ J 1 0 8 3

Bid two no-trump. You plan to pass if partner shows a minimum by rebidding three hearts. You will bid three no-trump if partner shows a club feature. You'll try four hearts if partner shows a spade or diamond feature.

Note that a two-no-trump response followed by three no-trump invites partner to choose between game in no-trump and game in his suit. The immediate three-no-trump response, as in the previous example, tells partner to let you play the hand there.

♠ A 6 4   ♡ J 7   ◊ A K Q J 1 0   ♣ A 3 2

Bid two no-trump. If partner happens to rebid three no-trump, showing a solid suit, go to seven no-trump—you can count 13 tricks. If he shows a feature, you can invite a slam or bid a slam. If partner shows a minimum, settle for game.

♠ A K 3   ♡ 5   ◇ K 5 3   ♣ A J 8 7 5 2

Bid three clubs. You hope opener can raise.

♠ A Q 4   ♡ 4   ◇ K J 7 5 4 2   ♣ K 4 3

Pass. Game is very unlikely, and there is no assurance that three diamonds is better than two hearts.

Responding to Preemptive Openings

Remember, your partner has suggested a number of tricks equal to *two less* than his bid when vulnerable, *three less* than his bid when not vulnerable. If your partner opens with three spades, vulnerable, you are justified in raising to four spades with

♠ 8　♡ A K 5 4 3　♢ A 7 6 5　♣ Q 6 5

You expect partner to have about seven winners, and you have three. Note that no special support for partner's suit is required.

Slam usually is out of reach after an opening preempt. The preemptor has little or no outside strength, and his hand may be worthless unless his suit is trumps. You shouldn't even think about slam unless you have first-round control (the ace or a void) in two of the other suits, at least second-round control (the king or a singleton) in the third suit and an ample supply of high cards to assure the necessary number of winners.

Three-level preempts in a minor suit present a particular problem. Many times there will be three no-trump in the hand while five of partner's minor cannot be made. If your partner opens three clubs or three diamonds, you should prefer to bid three no-trump if you want to try a game. However, you need (1) three or more fast tricks, including stoppers in all the other suits; (2) a fit for partner's suit. You should have at least two small cards in his suit, and preferably A-x or K-x. Otherwise, you may not be able to reach dummy enough times to establish and cash out his long cards. (Remember, partner typically will hold K-Q-J-10-5-4-2 of his suit and *no* outside strength.)

Even if you try three no-trump, your partner still can bid four or five of the minor with a hand that is very unsuitable for no-trump.

Rebids by Opener

After you have opened the bidding and your partner has responded, you must decide what to do next. As a preliminary, adjust your point count up or down as follows:

1. If partner raised your suit,

add 1 extra point for each card you hold beyond five.
add 1 extra point for any singleton or void.

2. If partner bid a suit of his own,

your shortness in his suit becomes a liability. Disregard any distribution points you previously counted in partner's suit. However, *if you have three or more cards in partner's suit,*

add 1 extra point for each card beyond three.
add 1 extra point for any singleton or void.

AFTER A SINGLE RAISE IN A MAJOR SUIT

Partner's single raise shows 6–9 points in support of your suit. If your suit is a major, adjust your point count by adding for extra trump length, singletons, and voids as mentioned above. If your adjusted count is less than 17, pass—the combined count will be 25 or less. If the adjusted count is 17 or 18, try for game, usually by reraising to three of the major. If your adjusted count is 19 or more, bid game in your major suit.

In the following examples you have opened one spade and partner has raised to two spades.

♠ A K 8 5 3 ♡ A 8 3 ◇ 7 2 ♣ Q 7 4

Pass. You have the same 14 points you started with. Game is impossible.

♠ A K 8 5 3 2 ♡ A 8 6 ◇ 7 ♣ Q 7 4

You started with 15 points, and the raise allows you to add 1 point for the sixth trump and 1 for the singleton, making a total of 17. Rebid three spades, inviting game.

♠ A K 8 5 3 ♡ A 8 6 ◇ 7 2 ♣ A K 9

You have 19 points. Rebid four spades. Even if partner has a near-minimum 7-point hand, you still will total 26 points.

AFTER A SINGLE RAISE IN A MINOR SUIT

You should plan to pass a single raise in a minor suit unless you have a very powerful hand or see no-trump game possibilities. Remember, it takes 29 points to make an 11-trick game a worthwhile undertaking.

Here are some examples. You have opened one diamond, and partner has raised to two diamonds.

♠ A 8 ♡ K 5 3 ◇ A K 7 6 4 2 ♣ K 3

Your point count has risen from 19 to 20 because of your sixth diamond. There should be a play for five diamonds, but a three no-trump bid is a far better action. Nine tricks should wheel in.

♠ A8   ♡ Q64   ◇ KQ9652   ♣ A3

Your hand is worth about 18 points. Bid two no-trump. This shows interest in game—you would pass if not interested. Partner can raise to three no-trump with 8 or 9 points. With less he will pass or return to three diamonds.

♠ 86   ♡ J53   ◇ AKQ642   ♣ A3

Your point count has increased to 17, but a five-diamond contract is out of the question. While you have seven tricks at no-trump, the opponents are likely to take at least five tricks in the major suits before you can muster nine. The trouble with passing is that the opponents may back into the auction and take the contract away from you—if your partner is very weak, the opponents may even have a major suit game. We recommend a tactical three-diamond bid.

AFTER A DOUBLE RAISE IN A MAJOR SUIT

When partner double-raises your suit, showing 10–12 points in support, you adjust your point count just as you did after a single raise. Your adjusted count plus partner's 12-point maximum usually will produce 26. You are unlikely to pass a jump raise in a major.

Here are examples of rebids after a one-heart opening and a raise to three hearts.

♠ A94   ♡ AQ976   ◇ Q32   ♣ 64

Pass. Your hand is worth no more than 13 points, and partner has a maximum of 12.

♠ A94   ♡ AQ976   ◇ K432   ♣ 4

Bid four hearts. You had 15 points to start with. By adding 1 extra point for the singleton, you have 16. Even if partner has a minimum three-heart raise, 16 + 10 = 26.

♠ A J 4 ♡ A K 9 7 6 ◇ K Q J 2 ♣ 5

Try for a slam. This hand had 20 points to start. Now 1 point can be added for the singleton. If partner has a maximum, the points for slam are there. Note that you have first- or second-round control of all suits, so your hand is slam-oriented.

AFTER A DOUBLE RAISE IN A MINOR SUIT

Even if you opened on a three-card suit, a double raise in a minor offers possibilities for a no-trump game. However, though partner's raise shows 10–12 points in support of your minor, he only has to have 7 high-card points, so you need substantial high-card strength to play in no-trump. You will head for game in your minor only if your side could have a total of 29 points.

Here are examples after a one-club opening and a raise to three clubs:

♠ K 10 4 3 ♡ A Q 2 ◇ Q 8 3 ♣ Q J 4

Pass. Though you might have enough high cards to make three no-trump, it is much against the odds.

♠ K 4 ♡ A K ◇ J 6 5 3 ♣ K Q 6 5 2

Bid three no-trump.

♠ K 7 6 5 ♡ 2 ◇ A K J ♣ Q J 9 7 4

Bid three diamonds. Your hand is now worth 17 points with clubs as trumps, and a further bid is called for. You intend to bid four clubs if partner says three hearts, to pass if he tries three no-trump, or to bid five clubs over anything else.

AFTER A DOUBLE-JUMP RAISE IN A MAJOR SUIT

With a double-jump raise of your opening bid partner shows at least four-card support and excellent distribution. However, he doesn't have much in high cards. He hopes to make the contract, but his action also is *preemptive*—he wants to keep the opponents from bidding. With a powerful hand, including three aces (or two aces and either the king or a singleton in the other suit), you may invite slam. Otherwise, pass and avoid the harrowing things that can happen to reckless overbidders.

AFTER A NEW-SUIT RESPONSE AT THE ONE-LEVEL

We have little new to offer on rebids after a one-over-one response in a new suit. Experts seem to cope with this situation well enough, but the average bridge player frequently can't understand how to handle a response which ranges from 6 to 18 high-card points and can be based on a suit of almost any length.

On his first rebid opener assumes that responder's hand is near the minimum end of the scale and his suit is at most five cards long. If responder has a better hand or a longer, stronger suit, he can tell about it later.

Let's see what opener can do based on his own high-card strength:

With 13—15 points: Show a second suit if convenient.
Rebid a six-card suit or a strong five-carder.
Raise your partner's suit one level with at least three-card support.
Rebid one no-trump.

KEEP THE BIDDING LOW. Do not, for instance, open one diamond on a four-card suit and then, if partner responds one spade, rebid two hearts on another four-carder. This sequence, known as a "reverse," might land you at the three-level when both you and partner have minimum hands. You need extra strength to "reverse" in this fashion.

With 16—18 points: Show a second suit if convenient. (Opener's simple rebid in a new suit may be passed, but responder will bid again unless he is very weak.)
Jump in your first suit, but only with a good six- or seven-card suit. This is not a forcing bid but a highly invitational one.
Jump-raise partner's suit, but only with four-card support. This is not a forcing bid but a highly invitational one.
AVOID a one no-trump rebid, the simple rebid of your own suit, or the single raise of partner's suit.

With 19 points or more: Bid game in no-trump or in your own suit (with a self-sufficient suit) or in partner's suit (with four-card support). With exactly 19 points and balanced distribution your correct rebid is two no-trump, which is not quite forcing.

Here are some examples. You opened one club and received a one-heart response.

♠ 74   ♡ KJ2   ◇ K95   ♣ AQ762

Rebid two hearts. Prefer the raise to the rebid of your own five-card suit.

♠ AQ   ♡ 106   ◇ KJ73   ♣ AKJ94

Rebid two no-trump. You have 18 high-card points and are prepared for the lead of any suit except hearts.

♠ 5   ♡ 106   ◇ AJ3   ♣ AKQ10965

Rebid three clubs. You have enormous playing strength and hope to hear partner convert to three no-trump.

♠ Q4   ♡ KJ76   ◇ 54   ♣ AK765

Rebid two hearts.

♠ Q4   ♡ AK43   ◇ 65   ♣ AK432

Rebid three hearts.

♠ 5   ♡ KQ73   ◇ K2   ♣ AK8765

Rebid four hearts. You have magnificent trumps, and your hand is worth about 19 points in support of hearts.

♠ AK87   ♡ 32   ◇ K54   ♣ QJ93

Rebid one spade. This space-saving rebid might locate a spade fit.

♠ AK87   ♡ 43   ◇ K5   ♣ AQJ65

Rebid one spade. You have extra strength but you cannot jump to two spades—that would force the auction to game even opposite a minimum response.

♠ AK8 ♡ 2 ♢ KJ93 ♣ AKJ94

Rebid two diamonds, a "reverse." This shows extra strength and is absolutely forcing. You have enough high-card points to rebid two no-trump, but you should not do so with a singleton heart.

♠ KJ2 ♡ 954 ♢ K6 ♣ AQ1076

Rebid one no-trump. With a balanced minimum hand prefer this rebid to either two hearts or two clubs.

♠ K76 ♡ 3 ♢ A43 ♣ AQ10654

Rebid two clubs. This suggests a six-card or longer suit.

♠ AQ ♡ 109 ♢ KJ102 ♣ AK1094

Rebid two no-trump. You have only 17 high-card points, but you also hold three tens, two nines, and a five-card suit. You are well-prepared for either a spade or diamond lead.

♠ AQ2 ♡ 654 ♢ KJ5 ♣ AKQ2

Rebid two no-trump. You have 19 high-card points this time, but your hand lacks *body*. If partner has only 7 points, you aren't likely to score a game. If partner has 8 points or more, he will take you to game. Despite the extra high cards this hand is only slightly better than the previous hand.

♠ AKJ4 ♡ 43 ♢ A4 ♣ AQJ76

Jump to two spades. A *jump shift* by opener is forcing and promises that the values for game are in hand, now that responder has been able to act over the opening bid.

AFTER A NEW-SUIT RESPONSE AT THE TWO-LEVEL

One area in which Standard American has been slow to keep up with modern expert bidding is opener's rebid after a responder bids a new suit at the two-level. In the thirties a two-over-one response sometimes was made with a relatively weak hand. As time passed, the minimum requirements were raised, and today this response shows at least 11 points. Even with a minimum opening bid opposite a minimum two-over-one response, you are close to game.

In the old days a two-no-trump rebid by opener showed at least 16 points. This treatment is no longer needed because today's experts are willing to open one no-trump on most balanced 16-point hands. In Jacoby the two-no-trump rebid shows a balanced *minimum* opening (a good 13–15 points) that is oriented well for no-trump play.

Another rebid that is treated differently today is a raise of partner's suit. It too used to show 16 points. Today it merely shows a sound minimum opening with support for partner's suit. If opener rebids his own suit at the two-level, that also shows a minimum.

In theory none of these minimum-showing rebids force responder to bid again. In practice responder seldom passes (especially if his suit has been raised), since his initial two-over-one response suggested the values at least to invite a game.

However, *jump* rebids below game by opener are forcing (for example, one heart—two clubs—three hearts). Even a *minimum* rebid in a *new* suit by opener could conceal quite a good hand, so responder always will find a further bid in that instance.

Here are some examples. You opened one spade and partner responded two diamonds.

♠ A Q J 7 6   ♡ 6 5 4   ◇ 5 4   ♣ A Q 3

Rebid two spades. Your hand is minimum and the good spade suit is your best feature.

♠ A Q J 7 4   ♡ K J 5 4   ◇ 5 4   ♣ A 2

Rebid two hearts. Your hand is worth 17 points and you definitely intend to get to game. However, you can save space by making a minimum rebid in your second suit—partner is forced to bid again.

♠ A Q 9 7 4   ♡ K J 2   ◇ 5 4   ♣ K J 5

Rebid two no-trump.

♠ A Q 9 7 4   ♡ 2   ◇ K J 2   ♣ K 7 6 5

Raise to three diamonds. Prefer this to a two-spade rebid— your partner will assume that you have at least five spades in any case.

♠ A Q J 1 0 7 6   ♡ 5 4   ◇ A 4   ♣ K Q 3

Jump to three spades to show a strong suit and extra high-card strength. This is a forcing bid.

♠ A Q J 5 4   ♡ A J 4   ◇ 5 4   ♣ A Q 3

Jump to three no-trump. (With 18 high-card points plus a five-card suit you were too strong to open one no-trump.) You are ready for any lead except a diamond.

AFTER A ONE-NO-TRUMP RESPONSE

Partner has shown 6–9 high-card points. He may be balanced or unbalanced, but he certainly doesn't have much support for your suit—often he will have only a singleton there. If you have . . .

13–15 points: Game is impossible $(15 + 9 = 24)$. Therefore, the object of any rebid is to get out of no-trump into a better spot. Rebid a six-card suit of your own or rebid two of a four- or five-card suit that ranks lower than the suit you opened. Otherwise, pass.

16–18 points: Game is possible, particularly if you have 18. If no-trump looks all right, raise to two. If you have a good six-card suit, jump to three of your suit. Otherwise, show a new suit and hope your partner bids again.

19 points or more: Bid game in your suit with a long, strong suit. Raise to three no-trump with a balanced hand, or jump in a new suit to force to game.

In the following examples you opened one heart and partner responded one no-trump.

♠ K74   ♥ AQJ63   ♦ K2   ♣ 862

Pass. You have a count of 14 (13 in high cards plus 1 for the doubleton). Do not rebid your five-card suit.

♠ K74   ♥ AQJ63   ♦ 2   ♣ K862

Rebid two clubs. You have the same high-card points as before, but a no-trump contract looks unsatisfactory. Show your other suit.

♠ K74 ♡ AQJ632 ◇ Q84 ♣ 4

Rebid two hearts.

♠ K74 ♡ AQJ632 ◇ AQ4 ♣ 4

Jump to three hearts. You have 18 points, including 16 in high cards. This is not a forcing bid, but it is a strong game invitation.

♠ A74 ♡ AQJ1092 ◇ 4 ♣ AQ8

Bid four hearts. Your hand is worth 21 points. In addition to the 17 high-card points and 2 distribution points for the singleton, you have a six-card suit that is worth 2 extra points—it will play well even opposite a singleton.

♠ AQ4 ♡ AKJ105 ◇ J3 ♣ A43

Bid three no-trump.

♠ A32 ♡ AKJ94 ◇ 3 ♣ AQJ3

Jump to three clubs. This jump shift is forcing to game.

AFTER A TWO-NO-TRUMP RESPONSE

Partner has shown a balanced hand, 13–15 high-card points, and stoppers in the unbid suits. The auction is forcing to game.

If you have 17 points or less, slam is unlikely. If your hand is balanced, just raise to three-no-trump and let partner have his fun.

If your hand is unbalanced, you may rebid a six-card suit or show a second suit of four cards or more. In these cases you are warning against no-trump. Partner should not insist on a three no-trump contract unless he has the unbid suits well under control.

If you have 18 or 19 points, you want to invite a slam. If your hand is balanced, issue your invitation by jumping to four no-trump. This particular four no-trump call is not Blackwood, just a raise of no-trump. If your hand is unbalanced, rebid in a suit and plan to make some try for slam later.

With 20 points or more make sure slam is reached.

Examples of opener's rebid after a one-spade opening and a two no-trump response:

♠ KJ875   ♡ Q2   ◇ AQ6   ♣ Q52

Rebid three no-trump.

♠ KJ543   ♡ 2   ◇ AKJ3   ♣ Q32

Rebid three diamonds. You hope partner will take a preference to three spades—you then can bid game in spades. If he rebids three no-trump, pass—he should have good hearts and clubs. If he raises diamonds, five diamonds should be a safer contract than three no-trump.

♠ AQ9765   ♡ AQ7   ◇ K63   ♣ 3

Your hand has only 15 high-card points but it looks good for slam. Rebid three spades. If partner goes to three no-trump, you will continue to four spades. If partner raises to four spades, you may try for slam with Blackwood.

♠ AKQJ87   ♡ AQ32   ◇ K4   ♣ 2

Rebid three hearts. You plan to use Blackwood later and get to six or seven unless your partner happens to have no aces.

AFTER A THREE-NO-TRUMP RESPONSE

Partner has shown 16–18 high-card points with very balanced distribution. With 15 points or less pass if your hand is balanced. If your hand is very unbalanced, rebid your suit or bid a new suit.

If you have 16 points or more, move toward slam by bidding a new suit or raising quantitatively to four no-trump.

The Language of Bidding

This short section really belongs at the start of the book since it deals with basic concepts.

The purpose of bidding is to exchange information with your partner. Each bid you make tells partner something about the strength and shape of your hand. Every player knows what he wants his bids to mean, but unless his partner also knows the intended meaning, the correct message isn't delivered.

FORCING AND NONFORCING BIDS

An important job for any partnership is deciding which bids are forcing and which are nonforcing. In our system there are two kinds of forcing bids:

1. The game force. This commits the partnership to game unless they decide to stop to double an opposing bid.
2. The one-round force. This merely requires partner to bid at least once more.

Naturally, a player who forces to game knows that the partnership has at least 26 points to work with. A one-round force says that, while the bidder may intend to go to game or slam eventually, for the present he merely is exploring.

Bids of a new suit are always exploratory. We have noted that a new-suit response at the one-level may be based on 7–17 points and almost any distribution. It is a one-round force. Opener doesn't know what may be coming next—he just makes his proper rebid, assuming that responder has a minimum or near-minimum, and waits to hear his partner's next action.

Bids in no-trump, raises of partner's suit, and rebids of one's own suit all show a limited amount of high-card strength—they imply that the bidder hasn't much more to tell about his hand.

Let's list some of the most common forcing bids.

Game forces:

1. A jump in a new suit.
2. A two no-trump response by an unpassed hand.
3. A reverse by responder.

One-round forces:

1. A new-suit response (including a bid in the fourth suit) by an unpassed hand.
2. A reverse by opener.
3. A bid of a new suit after another suit has been bid and raised.
4. A bid of a new suit by opener after a two-over-one response.
5. Artificial bids such as the Stayman and Blackwood conventions, or a cue-bid of a suit the opponents have bid.

We already mentioned the "reverse," but just in case you aren't sure what it is, we will define it here—it is a new-suit rebid which, because of its rank, keeps partner from returning conveniently to the suit you bid first.

Say you open one diamond and rebid two clubs over a major suit response by partner. If he thinks your side is better off in diamonds, he can take a diamond preference at the *two*-level. However, if you open one club and rebid two diamonds, responder must go to the *three*-level if he wants to return to clubs.

Since opener customarily shows his longest suit first, responder *often* wants to get the partnership back to opener's first suit—indeed, responder may have a clear preference. Therefore, if the partnership lands at the three-level because of opener's reverse, *opener* must have the extra strength needed to underwrite the three-level contract. So a reverse is always a strong bid—a reverse by the opening bidder shows at least 17 points.

Even a club bid may be a reverse. Suppose you open one spade and partner responds two hearts. Now if you bid three clubs, you have bypassed two spades.

An example of a reverse by *responder* is seen in this auction: one spade by opener, two-diamond response; two-spade rebid by opener, *three hearts* by responder. If opener wishes to take a diamond preference, he must do so at the four-level. A reverse by responder shows at least 13 points.

BIDS THAT ARE ALMOST FORCING

The only forcing response available to a passed hand is a jump in a new suit. (This bid suggests that responder's hand is suddenly worth an opening bid because he has a good fit for opener's suit.) Simple suit responses are no longer forcing, but when you make one, you don't want your partner to pass—it is up to him to make his normal rebid if he has a sound opening bid.

Similarly, a jump to two no-trump by a passed hand shows a balanced 11–12 high-card points. If opener has *anything* more than a minimum, he should go on. If he has nothing more, he should pass.

Single-jump raises by responder, which are invitational in Jacoby, still have the same meaning when made by a passed hand. Partner is expected to go on to game with any excuse— you don't want to get into the habit of stopping just below game.

FREE BIDS

If an opponent bids on your right, you always have the option of passing around to your partner and letting him make the next move. A *free bid* is one made *directly* over a bid by an opponent. Some players think that a free bid is always strong. It is nothing of the sort—it merely shows that your hand is not an absolute minimum.

You hold

♠ A43   ♡ 654   ◇ Q54   ♣ AK74

You open one club and partner responds one heart. If right-hand opponent passes, you must discharge your responsibility to rebid by saying one no-trump. However, if a one-spade overcall is made on your right, you may pass, showing nothing extra. If you rebid one no-trump *freely*, partner would expect a hand like

♠ AJ3   ♡ J54   ◇ Q54   ♣ AK104

If you have a fit for partner's suit, you should take the opportunity to raise him even though you have no extra high-card values—the term "free raise" really is meaningless.

BIDS THAT SIGN OFF

The best sign-off is a pass. With some partners that is the *only* sure way to sign off.

Take this auction: one-spade opening by partner, two-diamond response by you, two-no-trump rebid by partner. Now three diamonds by you shows long diamonds and a minimum two-level response—it asks partner to pass. With many partners you can sign off by rebidding your suit like this. However, if your partner is untrustworthy, he'll stubbornly go on to three no-trump over three diamonds. So your best move may be to pass two no-trump, which may save you a few points.

Of course, good partners, who know and respect your bidding system, always will observe a sign-off. For example, they will pass after they open one no-trump and you show weakness by responding with two of a suit.

Competitive Bidding

This is where we separate the sheep from the goats in bridge.

It's easy enough to do a good job of bidding when the opponents sit back and let you operate. You may do a little better or a little worse than the next player, but as long as you let your point-count guide you to the proper level, you usually will find yourself in a good contract.

When the enemy competes, the story is entirely different.

Suppose your opponents play and make two hearts. You may have lost nothing, but suppose you could have made two spades. Then you have lost a lot. At duplicate (tournament) bridge you would receive a very bad score. In rubber bridge you have lost 60 points below the line instead of gaining 60, and you also have put yourself under a lot of pressure to keep the enemy from fulfilling their partial on the next deal.

Say you have bid to four hearts and expect to make it. A nasty opponent bids four spades against you. You are certain he isn't bidding four spades because he thinks he can make that contract—he is sacrificing, trying to take your game away from you. Should you double him or carry the bidding further? If you can't make five hearts, you should double and take your sure profit, small though it might be. If you can make five hearts, you may do better to bid on.

Let's look at the other side of the coin. You overcall a one-heart opening with one spade. The player on your left bids two hearts, your partner says two spades and opener jumps to four hearts. Should you compete with four spades?

It depends. Of course, you bid four spades if you expect to make it. You also should go to four spades if you think the opponents will make four hearts, while you will be down only one (presumably doubled) at four spades if vulnerable, or down only one or two if not vulnerable. A 200- or 300-point penalty is a loss, but it is a big saving against an adverse vulnerable game. (You can go broke with savings like this, but you go broke a lot faster if you let the opponents play all their laydown games.)

Even a 500-point penalty can represent a saving against a *vulnerable* game, but the odds here are poor. It doesn't pay to concede 500 points to save a game when there is any chance to set the opponents' contract.

Any of these sacrifices gives you a shot at a big profit—some opponents won't stop to double you but will automatically bid one trick higher. Your four-spade call will make no difference against such players if five hearts makes. But if five hearts goes down one, your sacrifice will show a tremendous gain.

In the following examples neither side is vulnerable and the auction has proceeded:

WEST	NORTH	EAST	SOUTH
	1H	1S	
2H	2S	4H	?

South holds

♠ A Q 9 6 5   ♡ K 6 5   ◇ Q J 4   ♣ 4 3

Pass. The heart king is a sure defensive trick, but it may be worth nothing for offense (North could have a singleton heart). The same thing goes for the diamond holding. You might beat four hearts easily, while four spades doubled could go down three tricks or more.

♠ KQ10865   ♡ A32   ◇ J87   ♣ 3

This time bid four spades. You have an extra spade, which argues for declaring and against defending. Your heart ace is useful for offense. You have much less defensive strength than before.

The jump overcall formerly showed a strong hand in standard bidding. However, the chances to use it in that way were infrequent, and a valuable bid was wasted. Like many of today's experts, Jacoby employs the *weak jump overcall*. It is another bid that is both easy to use and effective.

Our other competitive methods are the same as in Standard American, and we will show them in action.

BIDDING AGAINST A SUIT OPENING

You don't have to compete when your right-hand opponent opens the bidding—you shouldn't, in fact, unless you have a good reason. Don't bid merely because you have 13, 14, or even 15 high-card points. While high cards are your first consideration in opening the bidding, distribution and playing strength must be your first consideration in entering the auction when the opponents have opened.

Some reasons to compete:

1. You want to start a campaign leading to a makable contract of your own.
2. You want to uncover a profitable sacrifice.
3. You want to indicate a line of defense against an expected opposing contract.
4. You want to crowd the bidding to make it hard for your opponents to get to their best contract.

The two most common methods of entering the auction are the overcall and the takeout double.

OVERCALLS

Though an overcall may contain an opening bid or better in high-card points, it is primarily a defensive measure. In many cases you expect the opponents will go ahead and play the hand somewhere.

When you overcall, you give the opponents an option—they may double you, penalizing you for getting into their auction. You seldom get doubled in a one-level overcall, but overcalls at the two-level are apt to be dangerous. In either instance the main requirement for an overcall is a playable suit—some certain tricks if your suit is trumps. With this in mind it is wise to have a five-card suit at the one-level and a six-card suit at the two-level.

THE SPADE SUIT IS BOSS

If you have spades, the highest-ranking suit, try to get in an overcall. With other suits it is a good policy not to risk a penalty of more than 500 points; but with the spade suit, which offers excellent competitive advantages, you should be more willing to take some chances.

YOUR HOLDING IN AN OPPONENT'S SUIT

The more cards you have in the suit your opponent opened, the less desirable it is to overcall. Your length in the opponent's suit is evidence of a possible misfit, and you may be better off out of the auction.

Cards in the opponent's suit, especially secondary honors, will work for you on defense. They won't work for you as declarer.

EXAMPLES OF OVERCALLS

♠ KJ976 ♡2 ◇K107 ♣A954

Bid one spade over an opposing opening in any suit and at any vulnerability. You are taking a chance, but you have spades.

♠876 ♡632 ◇AK4 ♣AK85

Don't overcall. This is the classic 1930 sucker overcall of two clubs. You have 14 high-card points and four quick tricks, but your hand will take four tricks whether you are declarer or a defender. Your best chance for a profit is to pass and hope the opponents get too high.

♠K95 ♡97 ◇AK1063 ♣742

Overcall a one-club opening with one diamond. Pass over a one-heart or one-spade opening. Your five-card suit is not strong enough to warrant action at the two-level.

♠AQ1084 ♡K32 ◇54 ♣AQ10

Overcall any suit opening with one spade. This is a very good overcall—you hope your partner will find a bid so you can head for game.

♠AQ1084 ♡K732 ◇4 ♣AQ10

Overcall a one-heart or one-club opening with one spade. If the opening is one diamond, a takeout double is a strong alternative.

WEAK JUMP OVERCALLS

Back in 1931 Oswald Jacoby invented the weak jump overcall for use in the Culbertson-Lenz match. The bid is in general expert use today, and we use it in Jacoby. The bid does not always work, but sometimes it leads to a cheap sacrifice or jockeys the opponents out of their best contract.

Here are some examples:

♠ A Q J 7 6 5   ♡ 3 2   ◇ 7 4 3 2   ♣ 8

If not vulnerable, overcall any one-level suit opening with two spades. If you want to be a desperado, overcall even if vulnerable. Change the seven of spades to the ten and you definitely should.

♠ A Q J 7 6 5   ♡ A 3   ◇ 7 4 3   ♣ 8 2

Just overcall one spade. You can bid again if you get a good chance.

♠ 2   ♡ K 1 0 7 6   ◇ Q J 1 0 8 5 4 3   ♣ 2

If not vulnerable, overcall any suit opening with three diamonds. You may have a cheap save at a high level in diamonds. If not, you will have crowded the opponents.

PREEMPTIVE OVERCALLS

You still may preempt at a high level even though an opponent has opened the bidding. Suppose, at favorable vulnerability, you hold

♠ 8 5 4   ♡ 3   ◇ 8   ♣ A Q J 9 7 5 3 2

If you were the dealer, you would open four clubs or five clubs. If the bidding is opened on your right with one of a suit, a jump to four clubs or five clubs is still your best action.

THE TAKEOUT DOUBLE

This is a bread-and-butter call that gives you a chance to compete on equal terms with the opening bidder. Since it asks partner to bid a suit, the first test of a good takeout double is being prepared for any response partner may make.

The takeout double is an attacking call, so you prefer to have points with a singleton in the opponent's suit, or 13 high-card points with a doubleton. It also is advisable to have support for all the unbid suits (or a strong hand with a long suit of your own). Hence, the more cards you have in the opening bidder's suit, the less desirable a double—you seldom should double with three or more cards there.

Here are examples of possible takeout doubles:

♠ K J 96   ♡ A Q 104   ◊ 2   ♣ K 974

You have a classic sound double of a one-diamond opening. With good support for both majors you might also risk a double of one club. Over one heart or one spade you should pass.

♠ A Q 2   ♡ 76   ◊ K J 98   ♣ A 1074

Double a one-heart opening; pass over any other suit.

♠ A Q J 965   ♡ 2   ◊ K 54   ♣ A 72

Overcall a minor suit opening with one spade—do not consider a takeout double with a glaring weakness in one of the major suits. Over a one-heart opening a takeout double is possible. With a one-suited hand, however, prefer to overcall one spade.

♠ A Q J 96   ♡ 43   ◊ A Q 7   ♣ K Q 3

Over, say, a one-heart opening, double. If partner responds with two clubs or two diamonds, bid two spades at your next turn. You show a strong hand (at least 17 high-card points) and at least a five-card suit. With less strength you merely would have overcalled one spade at your first turn.

THE ONE NO-TRUMP OVERCALL

This bid shows a one no-trump opening with at least one stopper in opener's suit. With

♠ KJ65　♡ A2　◇ KJ8　♣ AJ43

you have 17 high-card points and should overcall a one-spade, one-diamond, or one-club opening with one no-trump. You should prefer to double a one-heart opening.

Other Competitive Situations

RESPONDING TO PARTNER'S OVERCALL

You raise an overcall as if it were an opening bid, but with one difference—you assume that the overcall is based on at least a five-card suit (at the two-level or higher, a six-card suit). Hence, you always can afford to raise an overcall with just three trumps.

A one-no-trump response to an overcall shows a better hand than the same response to an opening bid—about 8–11 high-card points with a guaranteed stopper in the opponent's suit. A two-no-trump response shows 12–14 high-card points; three no-trump shows 15–17.

A new-suit bid is not a force. In fact, it implies lack of interest in overcaller's suit. A jump in a new suit is highly invitational but not quite forcing.

How do you force partner? You cue-bid the opponent's suit. This kind of cue-bid doesn't guarantee first- or even second-round control of the opponent's suit—it merely shows a very good hand and asks partner to tell more about his overcall.

Jump raises may be played as limited and invitational, the same as in responding to an opening bid. However, since a cue-bid of the opponent's suit is available to show any good hand, an alternative is to play a jump raise as *preemptive*.

Here are some examples of responding to an overcall:

♠ K84 ♡ A97 ◇ 32 ♣ J9654

Raise partner's one-heart or one-spade overcall to two. Bid one no-trump if partner overcalled a one-club opening with one diamond.

♠ KJ1084 ♡ 2 ◇ K9765 ♣ 32

If partner overcalled one spade, raise directly to game. He may not make it, but you are making it very difficult for the opponents to compete. Bid one spade over partner's one-heart overcall.

♠ KJ854 ♡ K97 ◇ 2 ♣ A843

If partner overcalls a one-diamond opening with one heart, bid three hearts if that is invitational to game. Otherwise cue-bid two diamonds. If partner overcalls with one spade, you certainly should cue-bid two diamonds. You plan to bid at least four spades later. If partner holds as little as

♠ A9732 ♡ AQ3 ◇ 7653 ♣ 2

you have a fine play for slam.

RESPONDING TO PARTNER'S TAKEOUT DOUBLE

When partner makes a takeout double, he asks you to bid. Don't pass from fright with a weak hand. It is too costly to let your opponents make a doubled contract (possibly with over-tricks) even if it doesn't give them game. The only time to pass is when you are very strong in the suit doubled.

Most of the time you will have 9 points or less, and you should bid a suit at the minimum level. Prefer a major suit to a minor, but don't distort your hand for this reason.

With 10–12 points and a decent suit respond with a jump. This jump bid is not forcing but invites game.

With more than 12 points plan to bid a game. You can jump to a game yourself with a good notion of the best contract. If in doubt, you can force partner by cue-bidding the opening bidder's suit.

Responses in no-trump show balanced distribution, a stopper in the opening bidder's suit, and high-card values. Do *not* respond in no-trump with a bust. With 8–10 high-card points bid one no-trump; with 11–12 bid two no-trump (invitational to game); with more, jump to game in no-trump or cue-bid.

Here are some examples of responding to a takeout double.

♠ 7654   ♡ 543   ◊ 43   ♣ 8432

Respond two clubs to a double of one spade, and one spade to a double of any other suit. Hope that lightning won't strike. When you have a hand this weak, opening bidder's partner may bid over your partner's double, relieving you of the obligation to respond.

♠ J965   ♡ 32   ◊ 652   ♣ AJ74

Respond two clubs to a double of one spade—you are slightly too weak to respond one no-trump. Respond one spade to a double of any other suit.

♠ K1065   ♡ AQ9   ◊ J93   ♣ 765

Respond one no-trump if partner doubled one spade. Respond one no-trump or jump to two spades if partner doubled one heart. Jump to two spades if partner doubled one club or one diamond.

♠ 65   ♡ QJ1098   ◊ AK7   ♣ K83

If the opening bid was one spade, diamond, or club, show your great strength by cue-bidding two of opener's suit. If the opening bid was one heart, pass.

REBIDDING AFTER DOUBLING

If partner responds with a minimum bid, pass unless you have at least an ace better than a minimum takeout double. Jump only if you have a tremendous hand—remember, your partner could have no points at all. If you want to force partner, cue-bid the enemy suit.

Here are examples of rebids after a takeout double. One heart was opened in front of you, you doubled, and partner responded one spade.

$$\spadesuit KQ43 \quad \heartsuit 76 \quad \diamondsuit A54 \quad \clubsuit AJ43$$

Pass. If partner is very weak, even one spade is going down.

$$\spadesuit KQ43 \quad \heartsuit 76 \quad \diamondsuit AK3 \quad \clubsuit AJ43$$

Raise to two spades. Game is barely possible if partner has a maximum one-spade response, with close to 9 points.

$$\spadesuit KQ43 \quad \heartsuit 3 \quad \diamondsuit AKQ3 \quad \clubsuit AJ43$$

Raise to three spades. If partner has a trick in his hand, he should go on to game.

$$\spadesuit A102 \quad \heartsuit 43 \quad \diamondsuit AQ3 \quad \clubsuit AKJ43$$

Bid two clubs. You would have overcalled two clubs at your first turn with a club suit and only a fair hand. This sequence shows a strong hand and a strong suit.

BIDDING OVER AN OPENING ONE NO-TRUMP

Most of the time you will pass—with your opponent having advertised 16–18 high-card points, it will be too dangerous to bid. If you do bid, be careful—you must have a long, strong suit as protection.

Here are example hands. With neither side vulnerable your right-hand opponent opened one no-trump.

♠ Q54 ♡ AQ753 ◇ A54 ♣ J3

Pass. A two-heart overcall on a poor suit and scattered high-card strength risks a big set and has little to gain.

♠ QJ10965 ♡ 7 ◇ QJ105 ♣ A3

Bid two spades.

♠ KQJ1086 ♡ A3 ◇ A54 ♣ 43

Double. On the lead of the king of spades you have one no-trump beaten in your own hand.

BIDDING OVER AN OPPONENT'S WEAK TWO-BID

Opener has crowded you by using this bid, but he also has shown weakness. Tend to bid as though your opponent had opened one, except that you must act a level higher.

Here are some examples. With neither side vulnerable your right-hand opponent dealt and opened two hearts.

♠ K765 ♡ 65 ◇ AQ87 ♣ AJ3

Double.

♠ AKJ87 ♡ 65 ◇ KJ82 ♣ Q2

Overcall two spades.

♠ A3 ♡ K54 ◇ KJ10876 ♣ K3

Overcall three diamonds. A little more discretion is called for at the three level.

♠ A3 ♡ KJ3 ◇ AKJ2 ♣ J1076

Overcall two no-trump. This shows the same hand as a one no-trump overcall of a one-bid.

♠ A54 ♡ QJ5 ◇ AQ542 ♣ J4

Pass. It is too dangerous to act—your hand is defensive in nature.

WHEN YOUR PARTNER'S OPENING BID IS DOUBLED FOR TAKEOUT

When second hand doubles your partner's opening bid, you have one easy way to let partner know that your side holds the balance of power—you redouble.

This redouble shows at least 9 high-card points and is the correct action on all really strong hands. By redoubling you promise partner that you will not let the bidding die if it comes back to you—you might be planning to double an opposing bid, raise partner's suit, or bid a new suit.

Other actions over a takeout double are limited in strength. However, you do not always redouble just because you have 9 high-card points—it still is desirable to treat a new-suit response at the one-level as forcing. Bids at the two-level become sign-offs, telling partner that you have a bad hand with a long suit (usually at least six cards).

Jump raises are weaker than normal, since a 10-point hand with support in partner's suit will begin with a redouble.

Examples of responder's action after partner's one-heart opening bid is doubled:

♠ K J 9 7 5   ♡ 2   ◊ Q 8 6 4   ♣ K 8 7

Bid one spade.

♠ J 9 6 2   ♡ 8 5   ◊ A J 8 7   ♣ Q 10 7

Bid one no-trump.

♠ Q J 10 9 7 6   ♡ 2   ◊ K 3 2   ♣ 5 4 3

Bid two spades. Over a takeout double a jump shift becomes a *preemptive* bid. With a strong hand you would redouble.

♠ K 6   ♡ Q 8 7 4   ◊ J 10 5 4 3   ♣ 6 2

Bid three hearts. This is also a *preemptive* action.

♠ 7 5 4   ♡ 2   ◊ K Q 10 8 6 5   ♣ 5 4 3

Bid two diamonds. This bid shows weakness.

♠ A 4   ♡ K Q 5   ◊ Q 6 5 4 3   ♣ 4 3 2

Redouble, planning to support partner's hearts at the minimum level at your next turn.

♠ K 6   ♡ A Q 7 4   ◊ K 10 5 4 3   ♣ 6 2

Redouble. You are on your way to game in hearts in spite of the double.

♠ K J 5 4 2   ♡ 5 2   ◊ A Q 8 7   ♣ Q 3

Redouble. If the opponents escape to spades or diamonds, double them for penalty. If they run to clubs, maybe partner will be able to double, having heard about your strength.

WHEN *YOUR* OPENING BID IS DOUBLED FOR TAKEOUT

If your partner bids a new suit at the one-level, make your normal rebid. If he passes, be careful about reentering the auction—partner may be very weak or may lack support for your suit.

If partner responds at the two-level in a new suit, his bid shows weakness. Pass without extra strength, especially if you have no fit for partner's suit.

Balancing

When an opening bid of one of a suit on your left is followed by two passes, your right-hand opponent is marked with a poor hand. Since your partner may well have good cards, you should reopen the bidding with any excuse. (Partner may have passed even with substantial high-card values because he had no ideal action available. For example, he might have had length and strength in the opening bidder's suit.)

The minimum strength for a so-called *balancing* overcall is much less than the strength needed for the same action in the *direct* position. The range for a one-no-trump overcall, for instance, is reduced to 11–14 high-card points. The requirements for a takeout double also are reduced, even though you still tend to use a takeout double any time you have a good hand—sometimes your partner will have a good holding in opener's suit and he will convert your takeout double to penalty by passing.

Jump overcalls in the balancing position are no longer preemptive—instead, they are *intermediate,* showing a good six- or seven-card suit and a sound opening bid.

Examples, after a one-heart opening on your left is passed around to you:

♠ K87 ♡ QJ54 ◇ K103 ♣ A75

Bid one no-trump.

♠ A Q 9 6 4   ♡ 3 2   ◇ 8 5 4   ♣ J 4 2

Bid one spade.

♠ K 1 0 6   ♡ 4 3 2   ◇ A Q 1 0 6 4   ♣ 8 7

Bid two diamonds.

♠ A 1 0 7 6   ♡ 4 3   ◇ A Q 1 0 6   ♣ J 5 4

Double. You will be delighted if partner leaves this double in.

♠ K 1 0 7   ♡ 6 5   ◇ A Q J 8 7   ♣ A 3 2

Double. If partner responds one spade or two clubs, you will bid two diamonds, confirming that you have a sound takeout double and weren't balancing with a shaded one.

♠ A K Q J 9 8   ♡ 2   ◇ 8 5 4   ♣ J 4 2

Jump to two spades, intermediate.

OTHER BALANCING BIDS

When the opponents locate a trump fit but stop in a low part-score, you almost always should back into the auction with a bid or a takeout double. Your side will hold about half the high-card strength, and since the opponents have located a trump suit, your side also rates to have a fit somewhere. As always, your objective in balancing is to push the opponents up a little higher where they may go down.

Suppose the auction has gone:

	NORTH	
WEST	Pass	EAST
2 ♡		1 ♡
		Pass
	SOUTH	
	Pass	
	?	

You, South, have

♠ Q653   ♡ 54   ◇ AJ5   ♣ K542

Double. You weren't quite strong enough to double one heart, but you should balance with a double now. *It is losing tactics to let the opponents play comfortably when they find a trump suit but stop at the two-level.*

♠ QJ1065   ♡ 654   ◇ AJ4   ♣ 87

Bid two spades. Partner, of course, must realize that you *expect* him to hold some high cards when you balance in this situation—he must not go wild and bid game just because he has about an opening bid. He must remember that you passed at your first turn.

WHEN NOT TO BALANCE

Don't balance when the opponents haven't found a fit.

	NORTH	
	Pass	
	Pass	
WEST		EAST
1 ♡		1 ◇
2 ♡		2 ◇
		Pass
	SOUTH	
	Pass	
	Pass	

South holds:

♠ Q 10 9 6 5   ♡ Q 5   ◇ A J 4   ♣ 8 7 2

If you bid two spades this time, you are asking for trouble. There is no guarantee that partner has spade support or much high-card help—the opponents could have stopped low simply because they sensed a misfit. If you are declarer, your queen of hearts will be worthless.

Slam Bidding

Slam bidding is a lot of fun, and successful slams mean money in the bank. Good slam bidding, though, means more than just bidding and making slams—it means being disciplined enough to stay out of bad slams. Also, it is important to stop right at game when you don't go to six—there is nothing more frustrating than bidding to the five-level in pursuit of a slam and going down there.

Good slam bidders try to investigate slam possibilities early in the auction—they try to tell partner about their slam interest while still below game. When a good slam bidder goes past game, he is certain that the five-level is safe. He is prepared to reach slam unless partner warns him that slam is impossible.

THE BLACKWOOD CONVENTION

You can't make a slam if the opponents cash two aces before you take your own tricks. The Blackwood convention (invented in 1934 by Easley Blackwood of Indianapolis) is a method of finding out how many aces your partner holds. Everyone plays Blackwood (or some variation of it) today, but just for the record, here's how it works:

In many situations a bid of four no-trump is artificial and forcing. Partner responds as follows:

With no aces or all four aces ...... five clubs
With one ace .... five diamonds
With two aces.................... five hearts
With three aces .... five spades

In the convention's original form a five-no-trump response was used to show all four aces. It didn't take Easley and other expert users of Blackwood long to see that a player easily could tell just by looking at his own hand whether a five-club response showed no aces or all four.

There is a possible follow-up to Blackwood. If your partner's response reveals that your side holds all four aces, you may continue by bidding five no-trump to ask for kings. Partner's responses follow the same schedule, except that a six-club response shows no kings. (If he has four kings, he can bid seven of your agreed trump suit himself on the theory that you would not be asking for kings unless you were sure of seven if your side had all four of them. Alternatively, partner can respond six no-trump to show four kings.)

Contrary to popular belief, Blackwood is really not a slam-*bidding* method at all—it is a way to avoid bad slams. It is a final check to make sure you have enough aces for a slam after you have learned that there are enough playing tricks, good trumps, and controls (first-round control of three suits and at least second-round control of the fourth) to make slam a possibility. In other words, you should not use Blackwood unless you intend to bid six if partner's response confirms that your side holds three of the four aces.

You also should know just what to do after a response indicating that you have all four aces. Possibly you will be ready to go to seven, perhaps you intend to stop at six, or maybe you plan to explore grand-slam possibilities by bidding five no-trump—*but you should have your plans made before using the convention.*

Therefore, the ideal hand for Blackwood is one on which all you care about is how many aces your partner holds. Suppose partner opens one spade and you are looking at

♠ A K J 7 4   ♡ A K J 6 5 3   ◇ 2   ♣ 4

It is possible, though unlikely, that your partner has no aces at all—in that case five spades should be a safe contract. If partner shows one ace, you belong in six spades. If he has two, you intend to bid a grand slam. Blackwood solves your problems.

Let's look at a slightly different hand.

♠ A K J 7 4   ♡ A K J 9 8 5   ◇ 3 2   ♣ Void

If partner opens one spade, you still want to be in seven opposite two aces. However, if partner holds this sound opening:

♠ Q 10 9 6 5   ♡ Q   ◇ Q J 10 7   ♣ A K J

a diamond lead will beat even a small slam.

Give partner another hand, a bare minimum opening bid this time but with the ace of *diamonds:*

♠ Q 10 9 6 5   ♡ Q   ◇ A 9 7 4   ♣ K J 3

Now you belong in seven again.

Clearly, Blackwood isn't the answer here—if partner shows one ace, you won't know which one it is.

In general, *don't* use Blackwood when

(1) you have a void;
(2) you have a worthless doubleton in an unbid suit.

Luckily, there is no law that requires you to use Blackwood before bidding a slam. For two alternative methods of bidding slams, see page 124.

INTERFERENCE WITH BLACKWOOD

Your partner bids four no-trump and the next player bids something. How do you show your aces? There are several playable methods. Jacoby uses a very simple one.

You double to show no aces, pass to show one, bid the cheapest suit to show two and the next-cheapest suit to show three. If your opponent has been kind enough to interfere with a five-club or five-diamond call, you won't be inconvenienced very much at all. If your agreed suit is spades, even a five-heart bid won't shut you out.

Suppose an opponent really jams you by bidding, say, six spades over partner's four no-trump. If you elect to bid, you are at the seven-level right then. In these situations a pass is encouraging—it says, "I am interested in seven." A double says, "I don't think we can make seven."

SHOWING A VOID WHEN PARTNER USES BLACKWOOD

The Jacoby method of responding to Blackwood with a void and one ace is to jump to six of your void suit—provided you think your void will be useful to partner (not duplicated by high-card values in his hand). Thus, if you open one diamond on

♠ K J 7 6   ♡ Void   ♢ A K 1 0 8 5   ♣ Q 1 0 5 4

and partner responds one spade, you would jump to three spades. Should partner go right to Blackwood, you would respond *six hearts*. However, if partner cue-bid four hearts and, after you returned to four spades, bid four no-trump, you would just bid five diamonds. Partner clearly has high cards in hearts (probably including the ace), so you wouldn't consider your heart void a working feature.

To show two aces and a useful void, respond *five no-trump* to partner's Blackwood four no-trump.

WHEN RESPONDER SHOULD TAKE CONTROL

When your partner asks for aces by bidding four no-trump, you must tell the truth about your aces. Don't lie because you are afraid of getting too high. Trust your partner!

Whenever your partner continues with five no-trump, he implies interest in a grand slam. You are supposed to tell about your kings, but if you can see that seven will make, don't take any chances—just bid seven yourself. For instance, you open one club with

♠ 65   ♡ KQ87   ◇ 3   ♣ AKQ962

and raise partner's one-heart response to three hearts. Partner bids four no-trump, you reply five diamonds. Now partner bids five no-trump. You can bid six hearts to show two kings, but partner might pass there. You can see that you hold the two key kings as well as the queen of trumps and a solid club suit. You should bid seven hearts.

WHEN IS FOUR NO-TRUMP NOT BLACKWOOD?

The simplest rule is to use all four-no-trump bids as ace-asking, but that is a poor way to play.

Sometimes you will prefer to bid four-no-trump in competition rather than five of a suit. Suppose your side has stopped at three no-trump after finding a fit in diamonds. An opponent bids four spades over you. With a spade stopper like K-x you may choose to bid four no-trump, playing for the ten-trick game, rather than five diamonds.

In Jacoby we also play that any four-no-trump bid made directly after partner has bid no-trump is a natural raise—this should be very easy to understand and remember. The most common instance is the direct raise of partner's one-no-trump opening to four no-trump. Here responder wants the hand to be played in no-trump and is interested in slam if opener has a maximum.

A four-no-trump bid also may be a natural raise if no suit has been agreed as trumps. Consider this auction:

OPENER	RESPONDER
1S	2D
2H	3C
3NT	4NT

Responder's last bid is natural—if he wanted to ask for aces, he just as easily could have done that on the previous round. Opener should pass or bid on, based on the overall strength of his hand.

THE GERBER CONVENTION

Gerber is a four-club ace-asking bid. It's not essential for you to play Gerber, but it will be a source of profit if you take the trouble to learn it.

In Jacoby a jump to four clubs over a one-no-trump or two-no-trump opening or over a two-no-trump response is artificial and asks for aces. (Remember, if partner opens one no-trump, Blackwood is unavailable—a raise to four no-trump is natural.) However, these are the only occasions we use four clubs as ace-asking—any other time, four clubs is more valuable as a natural bid.

Partner's replies are:

Four diamonds	no aces or four aces
Four hearts	one ace
Four spades	two aces
Four no-trump	three aces

Note that the number of aces shown by a Gerber response is always one *less* than the same suit response to Blackwood.

Using Gerber, if you follow four clubs with five clubs, you are asking for kings.

OTHER SLAM-BIDDING METHODS

A good slam contract depends on winners, strong trumps, and controls. You worry about having enough aces only when these conditions are satisfied. Sometimes, when you know that aces are no problem, a direct leap to slam is a good gamble. One advantage in "blasting" directly into slam is that it gives the opponents less help with their opening lead than a slower, more revealing sequence.

You can blast into some slams on power. If partner opens one no-trump and you have a balanced hand with 17 high-card points, you bid six no-trump—there can be no problem with a lack of aces.

Suppose you have

♠ A Q J 8 7 3   ♡ Void   ◇ J 3   ♣ A Q 4 3 2

and partner opens one no-trump. You might jump straight to six spades. The trouble with a more delicate approach is that you are going to reach six spades most of the time. Why invite the opponents to lead a diamond? Even if a diamond lead is best for the defense, they may lead something else if you bid slam directly.

Now suppose you hold

♠ A K Q 6 5   ♡ K Q 5   ◇ 5 4   ♣ A Q 4

You open one spade, partner responds three spades. Again, you might do well with a direct leap to slam; but there is still another alternative, a go-slow approach to slam bidding called *cue-bidding*. In this method, once a trump suit is agreed on, subsequent suit-bids at or above the game level show interest in slam and promise a *control* (usually the ace or king of the suit; sometimes a void or singleton).

Cue-bidding has several advantages. You can show *specific* aces and kings. You can make slam tries without getting too high. But the biggest advantage is that *either* partner can decide to bid slam in the middle of a cue-bidding sequence.

In a Blackwood auction the four-no-trump bidder has to place the contract.

Here are two auctions that use cue-bidding—first to avoid a bad slam, then to reach a good one.

OPENER	RESPONDER
♠ A K Q 6 5	♠ J 9 3 2
♡ K Q 5	♡ A 4
◇ 5 4	◇ Q 9 3 2
♣ A Q 4	♣ K J 3

1 ♠	3 ♠
4 ♣	4 ♡
4 ♠	5 ♣
5 ♡	5 ♠
Pass	

Beginning with the second round of bidding, the conversation goes like this—Opener (4C): "I think we may have a slam and I have the ace of clubs." Responder (4H): "I have the ace of hearts." Opener (4S): "I'm willing to stop at game." Responder (5C): "I have the king of clubs and I still think slam is possible." Opener (5H): "I can't bid six spades but I do have the king of hearts." Responder (5S): "I can't bid a slam—I have nothing in diamonds."

OPENER	RESPONDER
♠ A K Q 6 5	♠ J 9 3 2
♡ K Q 5	♡ 4 3
◊ 5 4	◊ A K 7 6
♣ A Q 4	♣ K 8 7

1 ♠	3 ♠
4 ♣	4 ◊
4 ♠	5 ♣
6 ♠	Pass

The translation—Opener (4C): "I think we may have a slam and I have the ace of clubs." Responder (4D): "I have the ace of diamonds." Opener (4S): "I'm willing to stop at game." Responder (5C): "I'm still interested and I have the king of clubs." Opener (6S): "I think six spades will make."

The conversations in both these auctions are very informative. But if opener used Blackwood, responder would answer one ace on both hands!

SLAM SIGNALS BELOW GAME

A two-club opening always is a slam signal. So is an immediate jump shift by responder. Either of these bids alerts partner to slam possibilities early in the bidding.

On sequences that start with a series of exploratory bids, you may want to suggest a slam without going past game. One way to do this is to stop off for an unnecessary bid.

Suppose you hold

♠ A Q 8 7   ♡ K Q 3   ◊ A 8 6 4 2   ♣ 7

Your partner opens one club and you respond one diamond. When partner rebids one spade, you are interested in slam. However, you do not want to get past four spades if partner has an unsuitable minimum. How can you give him the slam message without risking the five-level?

You start by rebidding two hearts. This is a reverse, and as such it is forcing to game. Assume that partner next bids two no-trump. Now you jump to four spades.

Partner will realize that you were going to game in spades all along (obviously, you have four-card spade support), but you stopped to make an unnecessary bid for a reason—you are interested in bigger things. Your bidding also marks you with club shortness and good spades, so if partner has the right cards (fair trumps, no "wasted" honors in clubs opposite your singleton, and some help in diamonds), he will move toward slam. If his hand is

♠ K J 10 5   ♡ A 6 5   ◇ K 3   ♣ A 9 6 3

he will insist on at least a small slam. But if he holds

♠ K 9 4 3   ♡ A 5 4   ◇ Q 4   ♣ K Q J 4

he will put the brakes on at game.

SLAM BIDDING AFTER A TWO-CLUB OPENING

Over a two-club opening responder artificially shows his point count according to the schedule on page 50. After a two-diamond response opener will not look for slam unless he has a fantastic hand; a two-heart response may give him some encouragement; after a two-spade response there is an excellent chance for slam, and responses of two no-trump or three clubs practically guarantee one.

Whatever responder does, opener rebids to show what kind of two-club opening he has (see page 50). If he rebids cheaply in no-trump, he shows 23–24 high-card points and a balanced hand. With 6 points or less responder will think only of game unless he has very powerful distribution. With 7–9 points responder is interested in slam (with 9, very much so). With 10 points or more he definitely is going to bid a slam.

If opener rebids in a suit, responder can raise if he has support or show a good suit of his own. While these calls are encouraging, rebids in no-trump are discouraging. Thus, on this bidding sequence:

OPENER	RESPONDER
2C	2D
2H	2NT

opener has shown an old-fashioned strong two-heart opening. Responder's first call shows 0–3 high-card points. His second call implies that he probably has 0 or 1.

In any case, since responder has shown his point count immediately, opener may know right away whether slam is likely.

FORCING MAJOR SUIT RAISES

When you use limit single-jump raises in the major suits, you must find a new way to show a hand with four-card or better support for partner's major and 13 or more points (11 or more in high cards).

Experts have tried a number of new ways to show this kind of hand. Some use artificial four-club and four-diamond responses to show different types of strong major suit raises—this costs nothing because these responses are almost never used in their natural sense. Other players use a three-no-trump response as their forcing major suit raise. But these responses have a common defect—they crowd the bidding and make slam investigation difficult.

If you want to save space, you simply can respond in a new suit and follow with a jump raise of partner's major. Unfortunately, this method is imperfect also—first, partner won't know whether you have three- or four-card support; second, the direct forcing raise traditionally has emphasized the quality of responder's *trump support*—if you bid a side suit first, partner may think your suit is longer or stronger than it really is.

We think the best way to describe strong hands with good support for partner's major is with the Jacoby two-no-trump response, described under the next heading.

The Jacoby
Two-No-Trump Response

This bid is used only in response to a major suit opening. It is not used when responder is a passed hand. It takes the place of the traditional double raise that is forcing to game and shows four-card support or better for opener's major. Because this bid is not part of standard methods, you and your partner must agree in advance to play it. Remember, your opponents are entitled to be aware of your partnership's agreement.

The requirements for the Jacoby two-no-trump response are simple: four cards in partner's suit (rarely more than four); 13 points in support with not less than 11 high-card points. *There is no upper high-card-point limit*.

Because the bid gives the partnership a chance to explore for slam at a lower level, opener is expected to rebid as follows over the jump to two no-trump.

1. With a singleton he bids three of that suit.
2. With a void he jumps to four of the void suit. (However, if opener's suit is hearts and responder has a spade void, he should jump to four spades only with at least 14 high-card points. With less he should treat the spade void as a singleton and bid only three spades.)

3. With no singleton or void and with a minimum opening, he jumps to game. This says, "Partner, I'm not interested in slam."
4. With no singleton or void but with 14 or 15 high-card points, he bids three no-trump, conventionally announcing slightly more than a minimum opening.
5. With no singleton or void but with 16 or more high-card points, he rebids three of the agreed suit. This denies any significant distributional feature, but lets responder know that there may be enough high-card values for slam.

To decide whether he has a good opening, opener should take away a king. If he still would have opened the bidding, his hand is good enough to rebid three of the agreed suit.

LATER BIDDING

The key to later bidding lies in the ability to exchange information below game. When either partner feels that he knows the hands do not fit well for slam, he should sign off at four of the agreed suit. That may not stop partner from going on, but a warning will have been given.

Suppose your partner opens one spade and you hold

♠ K953   ♡ 8732   ◇ A4   ♣ KQ5

With 12 high-card points and a doubleton, you have a minimum two-no-trump response. Partner's rebid will determine how you will proceed. Suppose partner rebids three clubs, showing a singleton club. Now your king and queen of clubs are partially wasted values, so it would be sensible to sign off at four spades. If partner's rebid is three diamonds or three hearts, the combined hands may fit together very well. Now you would go slowly with three spades, hoping that opener could cue-bid the club ace and give you the opportunity to show the diamond ace. This is better than bidding four diamonds immediately, which would make it less convenient for opener to cue-bid five clubs.

Here are two minimum hands opener might have, each with a red singleton, that would offer a good play for slam.

♠ A 10 7 6 4 2 ♡ K Q ◇ 6 ♣ A 8 4 2

♠ A Q 10 6 2 ♡ 5 ◇ K J 8 ♣ A 9 7 3

On each of these hands, partner will show the ace of clubs over your three-spade rebid. (Remember, his rebid at the three-level already has shown a singleton.) When you show the diamond ace, he is justified in bidding beyond game. On the first hand he can cue-bid four hearts on his K-Q. In the second case he can bid five diamonds, showing the king. In both instances you then can bid the spade slam.

Let's look at a slightly better responding hand.

♠ K 10 6 4 ♡ K Q ◇ A 9 3 ♣ J 10 6 2

This is a 13-point hand with some ten-spots thrown in. If partner rebids three hearts, showing a singleton, you should sign off at four spades—your king and queen of hearts are 5 wasted points. However, rebids of three clubs or three diamonds by opener should encourage you. Over three clubs you will cue-bid the diamond ace. Over three diamonds you'll mark time with three spades, leaving partner room to cue-bid four clubs. You then can show the diamond ace.

It is important to remember that when responder or opener bids three of the agreed trump suit in the flow of constructive bidding, he does not deny holding a side ace or aces. Instead, he may be trying to save bidding room.

Let's look at two example auctions:

	OPENER	RESPONDER
1.	♠ A 9 8 6 5	♠ K 10 7 4 3
	♡ 10	♡ A 8 6 2
	◇ 9 8 5 2	◇ A K 5
	♣ A K 5	♣ 9

OPENER	RESPONDER
1 ♠	2NT
3 ♡	4NT
5 ♡	5NT
6 ◇	7 ♣

Opener rebids three hearts to show his singleton, and responder now can use Blackwood. After finding out that opener has a king in addition to his two aces, he can risk a grand slam. It would really be bad luck if opener's king was in hearts, his singleton, but even then opener might just hold the diamond queen. On the cards above, the grand slam will make unless trumps are divided 3-0 (only about a 22% chance of occurrence).

	OPENER	RESPONDER
2.	♠ Q 9 2	♠ K J 10
	♡ A Q 10 9 5 2	♡ K J 8 6 4
	◇ A Q J	◇ K 2
	♣ 5	♣ K Q J

1 ♡	2NT
3 ♣	3 ♡
4 ◇	4 ♡

Opener rebids three clubs, showing his singleton, and responder discounts his wasted clubs honors. However, he has plenty of other values, so he bids three hearts to suggest slam interest. Opener now cue-bids his diamond ace, but by doing so, he denies the ability to cue-bid a lower-ranking ace. So responder, knowing that both black aces are missing, signs off in four spades.

Of course, simple Blackwood would have allowed the partnership to stop at five hearts. But every now and then, one of the opponents would have six spades headed by the ace, and his partner would get a ruff to set a five-level contract.

All Kinds of Doubles

All doubles give your partner an option. When you double a low-level bid for penalty, your partner may decide to take it out—that is his privilege. Similarly, when you make a takeout double, your partner may judge to convert it to a penalty double by passing. However, a knowledgeable partner will know the meaning of your double and will try to follow your wishes.

TAKEOUT OR PENALTY?

A double of an opening bid of one of a suit is for takeout. Under no circumstances do you want partner to pass just because he has a bad hand—you want him to bid unless he has a very strong holding in opener's suit and can pass for penalty.

A double of a one-no-trump opening is for *penalty*. For this double you may have great high-card strength behind the no-trump opener. More often you will hold a long, strong suit plus a sure entry or two. If your partner has a balanced hand, he really should pass your double (even with no high-card strength)—you may have the contract set in your own hand. Also, since you promise support for no particular suit, partner may be set badly if he takes your double out. If partner has a weak, *unbalanced* hand, it is permissible for him to run to two of his long suit. Even then it may be better for him to pass.

A double of a weak two-bid or a preemptive three-bid is for takeout, but your partner doesn't need overwhelming strength in trumps to leave the double in. On this auction:

WEST	NORTH	EAST	SOUTH
3 ♠	Dbl	Pass	?

South should pass with

♠ Q J 8 2   ♡ J 5 4   ◊ J 5 4 3   ♣ 5 4

expecting three spades doubled to go down.

A double of a four-club or four-diamond opening is for takeout, but it's a double of a ten-trick contract. With a balanced hand partner sometimes will pass and try for a set.

A double of a four-heart opening is optional. Partner often will pass, but doubler should be prepared for a takeout (especially to four spades).

Doubles of openings of four spades and higher are for penalty. Doubler promises to set the contract. Though responder may take the double out if he thinks he can make a game or slam in his suit, he is on his own.

What other doubles are for takeout? Almost all doubles of suit contracts that are made (1) when it's your first chance to double that suit, and (2) when your partner has not bid, doubled or redoubled. (The biggest exceptions are low-level balancing doubles.) Most repeats of a previous takeout double also are for takeout.

EXAMPLES OF DOUBLES

♠ AQ987 ♡ 2 ◇ AQ103 ♣ KJ8

WEST	NORTH	EAST	SOUTH
2 ♡	Pass	Pass	?

A reopening takeout double is clearly indicated.

♠ KJ96 ♡ AQ104 ◇ 2 ♣ AJ74

WEST	NORTH	EAST	SOUTH
		1 ◇	Dbl
2 ◇	Pass	Pass	?

Double again (for takeout).

♠ 5 ♡ AJ76 ◇ KQ106 ♣ KJ32

WEST	NORTH	EAST	SOUTH
1 ♠	Pass	1NT	?

Double for takeout.

♠ 10653 ♡ AK65 ◇ 2 ♣ AQ106

WEST	NORTH	EAST	SOUTH
1 ◇	Pass	1 ♠	?

Double for takeout.

♠ 43 ♡ KJ96 ◇ AKJ3 ♣ A54

WEST	NORTH	EAST	SOUTH
		1 ♡	Pass
1NT	Pass	2 ♡	?

Double for penalty.

♠ K753 ♡ 65 ◇ AJ6 ♣ Q742

WEST	NORTH	EAST	SOUTH
		1 ♡	Pass
2 ♡	Pass	Pass	?

WEST	NORTH	EAST	SOUTH
1 ◇	Pass	1 ♡	Pass
2 ♡	Pass	Pass	?

Double in both situations. These balancing doubles are for takeout.

♠ Q5 ♡ KQJ1094 ◇ A54 ♣ K4

WEST	NORTH	EAST	SOUTH
			1 ♡
Pass	1 ♠	1NT	?

Double for penalty.

♠ Q1043 ♡ AK765 ◇ A3 ♣ J4

WEST	NORTH	EAST	SOUTH
			1 ♡
Dbl	Redbl	1 ♠	?

Double for penalty.

♠ 4 ♡ AK54 ◇ KJ83 ♣ K1054

WEST	NORTH	EAST	SOUTH
		1 ◇	Pass
1 ♠	Pass	1NT	?

Double. This is for takeout, showing hearts and clubs. However, you also suggest diamond length and strength because you failed to make a takeout double at your first turn. Partner sometimes will pass for penalty.

♠ A K 6 5   ♡ 6   ◇ K 5 4   ♣ A Q 6 5 2

WEST	NORTH	EAST	SOUTH
			1C
Dbl	Pass	1 ♡	?

Double for takeout.

SPECIAL TAKEOUT DOUBLES

Many modern experts change the meaning of some common doubles from penalty to takeout. It isn't vital to use these special doubles, but we will describe them briefly so you will know them if they are used against you.

The *negative* double is used by responder after his partner's opening bid is overcalled. Suppose South holds

♠ 6 5   ♡ K J 6 5   ◇ A J 1 0 5   ♣ 7 6 5

WEST	NORTH	EAST	SOUTH
	1 ♣	1 ♠	?

South would like to act, but he can't bid two clubs (no support), one no-trump (no spade stopper), or two diamonds or hearts (not enough points). If South passes and West raises spades, North and South may be shut out of the auction.

Playing negative doubles, South would double one spade *for takeout*. He suggests hearts and diamonds but not enough strength to bid at the two-level.

The *responsive* double is used after an overcall by *over-caller's* partner. Say South holds

♠ 5 4 2   ♡ A J 6 5   ◇ K Q 5 3   ♣ J 4

WEST	NORTH	EAST	SOUTH
1 ♠	2 ♣	2 ♠	?

Again, South would like to act, but he lacks a good bid. If North and South use responsive doubles, South could double here to show length in the unbid suits and a desire to compete.

Some partnerships use responsive doubles after a takeout double as well as an overcall, but the usual procedure in either case is to play responsive doubles only when the opponents have bid and raised a suit. If East had bid two *hearts* in the example above, a double by South would be for penalty.

Before you adopt any special doubles, you and your partner must agree ahead of time that you are going to use them. You should discuss them thoroughly. When your partner uses a double with a nonstandard meaning, be sure to let your opponents know. It is unethical to conceal private understandings from the opponents.

LEAD-DIRECTING DOUBLES

The double of an artificial bid (for example, a Stayman two-club bid or a five-diamond response to Blackwood) shows strength in that suit. It is made to direct a lead or, occasionally, to suggest a sacrifice.

Many doubles of three no-trump are lead directing:

—If your side hasn't bid and partner doubles three no-trump, he may be asking you to lead the first suit bid by dummy. (If dummy has rebid the suit a few times, make your normal lead instead.)

—If partner has bid a suit and doubles three no-trump, he asks you to lead his suit.

—If you have bid a suit and partner doubles three no-trump, he asks you to lead your suit.

—If partner doubles on a strong auction like one no-trump/three no-trump, lead your shortest or weakest suit—partner's double shows a long, strong suit, and he hopes you will lead it. Without the double you would be likely to lead some other suit.

THE LIGHTNER DOUBLE

This is a common-sense double. When the opponents reach a slam under their own steam, you will be happy to set them even one trick. Therefore, a double is made not so much to increase the size of the possible penalty, but to ask partner to make an unusual opening lead. Often, this will be the lead of the first suit that dummy bid.

You hold

♠ 632   ♡ Void   ◇ A K J 9 8 7   ♣ J 6 3 2

WEST	NORTH	EAST	SOUTH
		1 ♡	3 ◇
3 ♠	Pass	4 ♠	Pass
4NT	Pass	5 ◇	Pass
6 ♠	Pass	Pass	?

Double. You want a heart lead, and a Lightner double will get it for you.

PART TWO

THE PLAY OF THE CARDS

◇　♣　♡　♠

The main objective of bidding is to get to the right contract. Once the bidding is over, declarer's object is to make the contract. The defenders' object is to set him. If the contract is assured, declarer can afford to look around for overtricks; if setting the contract is certain, the defense can try to set it as many tricks as possible.

The two of trumps outranks the ace of any other suit. Hence, when declarer is in a suit contract, his main objective is to utilize his own small trumps (to take tricks, and to keep *control* of the play so he can safely establish and cash winners elsewhere), meanwhile keeping the defense's small trumps from taking tricks against him. On most hands declarer should plan to pull the outstanding trumps as soon as he can afford to. The defenders, in turn, seldom should lead trumps but should work to score a small trump or two before declarer can conveniently draw them. However, the defense occasionally may find it necessary to lead trumps to keep declarer from trumping his losers in dummy.

The Opening Lead

Play starts with the opening lead. There is a twofold problem here. First, you must choose the suit to lead; second, you must choose a specific card. For this purpose suits may be divided into three classes: long suits of four cards or more; short suits (a singleton or doubleton), and three-card suits (neither short nor long).

CHOICE OF SUITS

Against no-trump open a short suit only if your partner has bid it, or if the adverse bidding has indicated that your partner will have length in it. For example, if the opponents' bidding goes one no-trump/three no-trump and you have only a doubleton spade, you can expect your partner to have at least four spades, perhaps more—the opponents wouldn't be likely to pass up playing in an eight-card spade fit.

Against a suit contract you might open a short suit because you hope to be able to trump that suit before declarer can draw your trumps. This lead is most likely to work when you have a weak hand—your partner probably will have some high cards. Also, it helps if you have the ace or king of trumps for an entry, so declarer can't draw trumps before your side has a second chance to lead.

You open a long suit against no-trump because you hope to establish your long cards. When you have a five-card suit, the chances are that no one else will hold more than three cards in it. After three leads you will have two cards left that will be winners. (However, remember that you must have an entry somewhere so you can cash them.)

Even with a four-card suit there is a possible long-card winner. If the suit is divided 4-3-3-3, your fourth card will be the last one left after three leads. Against a suit contract you also might lead a long suit in the hope that your long cards eventually will force declarer to use up his trumps. (See page 208, the forcing defense.)

You open a three-card suit only if your partner has bid it or if there are good reasons not to lead any of your long or short suits.

The bidding is the principal influence on your choice of a suit for the opening lead. If your partner has bid a suit, it usually pays to lead it—when you lead partner's suit, you remain popular with him whether the lead works or not. When your partner has not bid a suit, lead an unbid suit. If you do lead a suit bid by the opponents, select one bid by dummy in preference to one bid by declarer.

Here are three illustrations of how listening to the bidding can indicate the best opening lead:

1. The auction:

WEST	NORTH	EAST	SOUTH
		1S	Pass
2H	Pass	2S	Pass
4S	All Pass		

You, South, hold:

♠ 874   ♡ J63   ◇ KJ32   ♣ J32

Lead diamonds. Dummy is likely to have a good, long heart suit, which declarer can establish for discards. Go out aggressively looking for tricks for your side while you have a chance.

2. The auction:

WEST	NORTH	EAST	SOUTH
		1H	Pass
1S	Pass	2H	All Pass

You, South, hold:

♠ Q J 10 8   ♡ K 6   ◇ Q 9 5 4 2   ♣ 8 7

Lead spades. Dummy won't have much trick-taking power this time, and the spade suit is no threat to provide discards when you have good ones yourself. This is *not* the time to be aggressive.

3. The auction:

WEST	NORTH	EAST	SOUTH
		1D	Pass
1S	Pass	2C	All Pass

You, South, hold:

K J 9 3   ♡ 8 7 3   ◇ K J 9 2   ♣ 9 2

Lead clubs. West has a weak hand and likes clubs better than diamonds. Trump leads may keep declarer from trumping losing diamonds in dummy. Note that you have a good diamond holding to protect.

CHOICE OF CARDS

An opening lead of the fourth-best from a long, broken suit is one of the plays that have been handed down to contract bridge from whist, through bid whist, and auction bridge. Time has shown that this is the best way to attack with a long, broken suit. (You prefer to lead a low card because you are hoping your partner can contribute a high card to the trick. The lead of your fourth-best card often tells partner something about your holding—for instance, the lead of the two suggests a four-card suit.)

If you hold certain high-card combinations, you lead one of the high cards in accordance with the following table:

YOU HOLD 3 OR MORE HEADED BY:	LEAD AGAINST NO-TRUMP:	LEAD AGAINST A SUIT CONTRACT:
1. A K Q or A K J	A	K
2. A K	fourth best	K
3. K Q J or K Q 10	K	K
4. K Q	K	K
5. A Q J	Q	A
6. Q J 10 or Q J 9	Q	Q
7. Q J	fourth best	Q
8. A J 10	J	A
9. K J 10, J 10 9 or J 10 8	J	J
10. J 10	fourth best	J
11. A 10 9	10	A
12. K 10 9, Q 10 9, 10 9 8 or 10 9 7	10	10
13. 9 8 7	9	9
14. K 9 8 7, Q 9 8 7 or J 9 8 7	fourth best*	fourth best*
15. A	fourth best	A

*The lead of the 9 formerly was favored by many good players. In some situations it makes life easier for partner.

In examples 4, 7, and 10, if your partner has bid the suit, lead the higher honor against no-trump, just as you would against a suit contract.

In examples 5, 8, 11, and 15, these ace-leads against a suit contract are undesirable. Aces are meant to capture the opponents' kings and queens. Unless the auction strongly suggests the lead of this suit, try to find some other suit to lead.

Bridge books are in agreement with the best expert practice when it comes to the correct opening lead from the following three-card combinations:

K̲Q5   Q̲J4   J̲106   K6̲4   Q73̲   J85̲

The underlined card is the correct lead.

However, when it comes to holdings such as 9-5-4, 8-6-2 or 6-5-3, there is considerable disagreement. Most books recommend leading the top card, especially against no-trump—this indicates your weakness in the suit. However, confusion can result against a suit contract—your partner may think you are leading from a doubleton and try to give you a ruff.

Another school believes in leading the middle card (and playing the higher card on the next round). This approach is called M-U-D, for "middle-up-down."

If you are leading a suit partner has bid and you have raised, it is safe to lead the top card. In other circumstances many experts lead the lowest card. We agree, and we recommend you normally lead low, provided your partner is aware of your preference and understands what you are doing.

When opening a doubleton, always lead the top card. In no-trump you are attacking what you hope is your partner's long suit, and you want to give him a chance to conserve his high cards. Against a suit contract you lead the top card so your partner will know you have a doubleton.

Later Defense

As you play, keep in mind that you are trying to *beat declarer's contract*. Counting your potential defensive tricks can be a big help.

Dlr: West
Vul: N-S

NORTH
♠ K J 10 8 4
♡ A J 8 4
♢ 4 2
♣ 8 5

WEST
♠ A 9
♡ 10 3
♢ A Q 8 5
♣ J 9 6 4 2

EAST
♠ 7 5 3 2
♡ 9
♢ J 10 7 6 3
♣ A 10 7

SOUTH
♠ Q 6
♡ K Q 7 6 5 2
♢ K 9
♣ K Q 3

Suppose you are East. South opened one heart after three passes, North raised to three hearts, and South carried on to four hearts. West chooses a trump lead, and declarer wins and draws another round. Next, the spade queen goes to West's ace. West shifts to a club, and you win.

To beat this contract, you need two more tricks. There are no more tricks to be had in the major suits, so West must hold either the diamond A-Q, or the diamond ace and the club king. You should return a diamond, which caters to both those holdings. A club return would be good enough only in the second case, and would give away the contract on the actual deal.

As a general rule, stick to playing the suit you led originally unless you clearly see that some other suit is preferable. If you keep shifting suits indiscriminately, you may be helping declarer. When you are returning partner's suit, the rule is to return your highest remaining card if you started with three cards, and your original fourth-best card if you started with four or more.

When you do attack a new suit, pick one that belongs to your side. Let declarer develop his own suits. (See pages 205–207, active and passive defense.)

DEFENSIVE SIGNALS

Declarer has the great advantage of being able to operate his own hand and the dummy as one group of 26 cards. The defense can reduce this advantage by the use of proper signals.

The most important defensive signal, called *attitude*, is that of playing a high card to indicate strength in the suit or a desire to have the suit led. The play of a low card is at best neutral, usually suggests weakness, and sometimes compels partner to lead some other suit.

In deciding whether your partner's card was meant to show strength or weakness, look to see what lower cards can be accounted for. Sometimes a four will be the highest card your partner has available, while other times an eight may be his lowest. (When you want to signal strength, do so with the highest card you can spare. When you want to signal weakness, play your lowest card, not just any low card.)

When leading a card which is part of a sequence, *lead the top card of the sequence*. Nowadays, some players lead the ace from a holding headed by the A-K—this is a departure from the traditional style of leading the king from K-Q as well as from A-K.

If your partner leads a suit and you have a sequence of cards from which to play, play the lowest:

```
                864
   K952                      QJ10
                A93
```

West leads the two of this suit. East's proper play is the ten. When this forces this ace, West will know that partner has the queen and jack as well.

However, when you have a sequence and wish to *signal* strength, you play the top card in your sequence, as though you were leading to the trick.

```
                A7
   K8652                     QJ4
                1093
```

West leads the five of this suit against South's no-trump contract. If dummy wins the ace, East should signal encouragement with the queen.

OTHER EXAMPLES OF ATTITUDE SIGNALS

Your partner opens the king of hearts against a spade contract. Dummy shows up with Q-5-3, and you hold the 8-2. You aren't strong in hearts, but you can trump the third round. Play the eight to ask your partner to continue. If you held J-10-8-2, you would be strong in the suit. Here, though, you would be unlikely to want your partner to continue the suit (setting up dummy's queen). Unless you thought that the lead of another suit would be even worse, you would discourage with the two.

Your partner opens the three of spades against a no-trump contract. Dummy shows up with K-2, and the king is played from dummy. You hold J-10-8. Signal with the jack, the top of your sequence. This shows a desire for further spade leads but denies the queen.

The attitude signal usually is applied when your side leads, but it also can be used in discarding

Dlr: South
Vul: Both

NORTH
♠ 9 8 4
♡ A 9
♢ A 8 6 5 3 2
♣ 6 4

WEST
♠ A 2
♡ Q J 1 0 4 2
♢ Q J 9
♣ 7 5 2

EAST
♠ K Q 1 0 7 6
♡ 8 3
♢ 1 0 7
♣ J 1 0 9 8

SOUTH
♠ J 5 3
♡ K 7 6 5
♢ K 4
♣ A K Q 3

Contract three no-trump by South
Opening lead· queen of hearts

East plays the heart three at trick one, discouraging, and South wins the king. South then cashes the diamond king, plays to the diamond ace and leads a third diamond. East should reason that the contract is unlikely to be beaten if declarer has the spade ace. East should therefore throw the ten of spades, begging for a spade shift.

On another occasion East might be able to discard his *lowest club* to get West to switch to spades. But here the lowest club East happens to have is the eight, which might be confusing.

OTHER SIGNALS

There are two other common defensive signals. One is the *distributional echo,* which is employed, in the absence of any need to show attitude, to tell partner *how many* cards you hold in a suit. In this signal, which generally is used when declarer is leading a suit, a high-low sequence of play shows an even number of cards and a low-high sequence shows an odd number.

The distributional echo is employed in a situation like this:

           KQJ103
952   A84
            76

South is playing a no-trump contract and has no side entry to the dummy. Clearly, the defenders want to take the ace of this suit the *second* time the suit is led. Therefore, if declarer leads the six toward dummy, West should play the two, showing an odd number of cards. East will know to duck the first lead and win the second.

If West's holding were 9-5, he would play the nine on the first round. Now East would hold up the ace *twice*.

The third type of signal, called *suit preference*, is less common. The play of an *unusually* high card is used to draw attention to another suit that is high-ranking, while the play of an unnecessarily low card shows interest in another suit that is low-ranking. One application of suit preference is seen here:

Dlr: North
Vul: N-S

NORTH
♠ K 5 4
♡ Q 3
◇ K 5 4
♣ K Q 10 6 3

WEST
♠ J 10 9 6
♡ 10 8 6 4
◇ J 10 9 6
♣ 8

EAST
♠ Q 8 7 3
♡ 7
◇ A 8 7 2
♣ A 9 5 2

SOUTH
♠ A 2
♡ A K J 9 5 2
◇ Q 3
♣ J 7 4

WEST	NORTH	EAST	SOUTH
	1C	Pass	1H
Pass	1NT	Pass	4H
All Pass			

West leads the eight of clubs to partner's ace and ruffs the club return. But how does he know which suit to play next? A diamond to East's ace will result in another ruff for the setting trick, but on a spade return declarer will take the rest.

Using the suit-preference signal, East would anticipate partner's problem and return the two of clubs at trick two. Since East has a choice of clubs to return, his play is useful as a signal. A *low* club return would ask West to lead a diamond next (a *low*-ranking suit). If East had the spade ace instead, he would lead his *highest* club at the second trick.

Declarer Play

If you are declarer, plan the play of the hand as soon as the dummy is exposed. In your planning follow the code word ARCH, in which:

A . . . . means ANALYZE the lead
R . . . . means REVIEW the bidding
C . . . . means COUNT your winners and losers, and
H . . . . means the all-important "HOW CAN I MAKE MY CONTRACT?"

The following hand illustrates how this is done in a simple no-trump contract. You are South, the declarer. The hands:

DUMMY
♠ Q 7
♡ J 10 9 3
◇ Q 6
♣ K Q J 7 2

DECLARER
♠ A 10 2
♡ K Q 2
◇ A K J 8
♣ 5 4 3

You opened the bidding with one no-trump, and after a Stayman inquiry your partner raised you to three no-trump. West opens the six of spades. There is no competitive bidding to review this time. The analysis of the lead indicates that it is fourth-best from a long suit (or, far less likely, the top of a worthless holding).

If you play the queen from dummy and East produces the king, you may be in trouble in the spade suit. But if you play low from dummy, it doesn't matter how the opposing spades lie—you eventually will take two spade tricks. So you play dummy's seven of spades. East puts in the jack, and you win the ace.

You now can count two tricks in spades, plus four in diamonds and three in hearts (after the heart ace is knocked out). Nine tricks are certain, provided you attack *hearts* before you lose control of the other suits.

Note that it would be dangerous to try to set up clubs instead of hearts. If East happened to have four clubs to the ace, you could get only two club tricks (eight tricks in all) before the defenders established their spades.

SECOND HAND LOW

You played low from dummy on the first trick. This is in accord with the tendency (also followed by the defenders) to play low as second hand unless there is some good reason to play high.

For an example of when second hand should play high, just take the ten of spades out of declarer's hand in the example just shown. To get any value from the queen of spades now, you must play it on the first round, hoping it will win. Otherwise, it will drop under the king on the next lead of the suit.

Finesses and Positional Play

Suppose you hold the ace and queen of spades, and dummy holds two small spades. If the player on your left leads a spade, you are certain to make both your ace and queen because you will be last to play to the trick.

If you lead the suit from your hand, you will make only one trick (unless the king luckily falls under your ace), so you certainly would prefer not to be the one to lead spades. If you must do so, your best play is to lead from dummy and play your queen after right-hand opponent follows low. This play, known as a finesse, will produce a second trick for you half the time—whenever the king is on your right.

Thus, a finesse is an attempt to make a low card do the work of a higher one. If it works, you have gained a trick. If it fails, you have lost nothing.

Suppose you hold A-J-10 and dummy holds three small cards. If you lead out your ace, you have wasted the power of your jack and ten. If you lead toward your hand and play the ten, you are likely to lose that trick to the queen or king. But if you lead the suit toward your hand a second time and play your jack, you probably will win two tricks. The actual odds in favor of taking two tricks with this *double finesse* are a trifle better than three to one in your favor.

Here is another hand to declare, with some possible finesses. Try it, using ARCH as a guide.

Dlr: West
Vul: None

NORTH
♠ K 6 4
♡ K 6 5 2
♢ K Q 10 3
♣ J 3

SOUTH
♠ A 8 5
♡ 7 4
♢ A 9 5 2
♣ A Q 6 4

WEST	NORTH	EAST	SOUTH
1S	Pass	Pass	1NT
Pass	3NT	All Pass	

West leads the queen of spades, indicating that his suit is headed by the Q-J-10 or Q-J-9. You and dummy have a total of 26 high-card points, so West should have all the missing high honors for his opening bid.

Assuming a 3-2 diamond break, you have seven top tricks and need two more. There is a possible finesse to take in clubs, but any finesse should be taken on the assumption it will win. On this deal West is known to have the club king. Instead, you should lead a low club *through West toward the jack.*

West will be on the spot. If he rises with the king, you have nine tricks. If West ducks, dummy's jack wins, which gets you up to eight tricks. Then you can come back to hand and lead up to the king of hearts (a finesse) to get a ninth. The full deal:

NORTH
♠ K 6 4
♡ K 6 5 2
♢ K Q 10 3
♣ J 3

WEST
♠ Q J 10 7 3
♡ A Q
♢ J 4
♣ K 10 9 5

EAST
♠ 9 2
♡ J 10 9 8 3
♢ 8 7 6
♣ 8 7 2

SOUTH
♠ A 8 5
♡ 7 4
♢ A 9 5 2
♣ A Q 6 4

Another practice deal:

Dlr: West
Vul: N-S

NORTH
♠ J 10 7 4
♡ Q J 2
♢ K Q J
♣ K 5 3

SOUTH
♠ A Q 9 3 2
♡ K 10
♢ 8 7 5
♣ A 8 4

WEST	NORTH	EAST	SOUTH
1C	Pass	Pass	1S
Pass	3S	Pass	4S
All Pass			

West leads the two of clubs. He has a four-card club suit, but not Q-J-10-x or Q-J-9-x. Again, the bidding marks West with all the missing high cards.

While at no-trump it is better to count sure winners, in a high-level suit contract a better perspective of the play is available by counting possible losers. Here there are four—the diamond and heart aces, a possible spade, and a possible club—but a heart discard can be set up for the club loser.

Timing is important. If declarer wins the opening lead and loses a finesse to the spade king in an effort to draw trumps, West will win and continue clubs, setting up a trick there before declarer has set up his hearts for a club discard.

Instead, declarer must win the club ace at trick one, cash the spade ace, and lead the king of hearts. If West ducks, another heart lead forces the ace. Now declarer can win the second club in dummy and take his discard on the good heart in the nick of time. Only then is it safe for him to lead a second trump. Here is the full deal:

NORTH
♠ J 10 7 4
♡ Q J 2
◇ K Q J
♣ K 5 3

WEST
♠ K 6 5
♡ A 9 8
◇ A 10 4
♣ Q 10 6 2

EAST
♠ 8
♡ 7 6 5 4 3
◇ 9 6 3 2
♣ J 9 7

SOUTH
♠ A Q 9 3 2
♡ K 10
◇ 8 7 5
♣ A 8 4

THE TWO-WAY FINESSE

Suppose you hold A-J-2 and dummy holds K-10-3. To make three tricks, try to guess which opponent holds the queen and finesse through that opponent. For example, if you think the queen is to your left, lead to dummy's ten. The alternative play for three tricks, cashing the ace and king in the hope that the queen will drop, is mathematically inferior when you have so few cards in the suit.

FINESSE OR PLAY FOR THE DROP?

The more cards you and dummy hold in a suit, the better the chance for a missing honor to drop. In some instances playing for the drop is more likely to succeed than a finesse. Here are the odds:

Missing	Finesse with	Play for the drop with
King	10 or fewer cards	11 or more cards
Queen	8 or fewer cards	9 or more cards
Jack	6 or fewer cards	7 or more cards

Obviously, being able to work out where the missing cards lie is better than relying on a table of rules—this is an important part of good bridge. Here is an illustration.

Dlr: East
Vul: N-S

NORTH
♠ K 9 6 3
♡ A 10 3
◇ K 10 3
♣ K 5 4

WEST
♠ 8 7
♡ 9 6 5 4
◇ Q 8 7 6
♣ J 10 3

EAST
♠ Q 5
♡ K 8 7
◇ 9 5 4
♣ A Q 9 8 7

SOUTH
♠ A J 10 4 2
♡ Q J 2
◇ A J 2
♣ 6 2

WEST	NORTH	EAST	SOUTH
		Pass	1S
Pass	3S	Pass	4S
All Pass			

West leads the jack of clubs against South's four-spade contract. Dummy's king covers, and East wins the ace and queen of clubs and continues with a low one that declarer trumps. Declarer cashes the king and ace of spades, drawing trumps, and loses a heart finesse to East's king. When East gets out safely with a heart, declarer must locate the queen of diamonds.

Fortunately, this presents no problem—if South has kept track of East's plays. East has showed 11 high-card points so far (club ace, club queen, spade queen, heart king) and failed to open the bidding. So West must have the diamond queen— if East had it, he would have opened.

PART THREE

SAMPLE HANDS

The following hands illustrate additional points of play and defense A study of them will help you pick up extra tricks occasionally. Sometimes these extra tricks will determine the success or failure of the contract In any case, they will mean additional points on your score

Declarer Play

ELIMINATION PLAY

In making this play you eliminate suits from your own hand and dummy so the defenders cannot lead them safely. Then you give up the lead, forcing a favorable return.

```
                    NORTH
                    ♠ K J 9 5 4
                    ♡ A Q
                    ◊ Q 9 8
                    ♣ A 10 5
       WEST                          EAST
       ♠ 7 3                         ♠ 2
       ♡ J 9 7 6 4                   ♡ K 10 8 2
       ◊ J 7 3                       ◊ 10 6 4 2
       ♣ Q 7 4                       ♣ 8 6 3 2
                    SOUTH
                    ♠ A Q 10 8 6
                    ♡ 5 3
                    ◊ A K 5
                    ♣ K J 9
```

Contract six spades by South
Opening lead six of hearts

South has a sure thing. He goes up with the ace of hearts and draws trumps. Then he plays all his diamonds and leads a heart. It doesn't matter which opponent wins the king of hearts, because he will have to give South the contract. If the opponent leads a club, that eliminates any guess for the queen. If the opponent leads a red card, South will trump in one hand and discard a club from the other.

When the hand actually was played, South finessed the queen of hearts on the opening lead. East won the king and returned hearts. Later, declarer misguessed the queen of clubs and went down in his slam.

There is an irony on this hand. If dummy had held a low heart instead of the queen, South would not have been able to finesse. He would have had a much better chance to spot the elimination play.

THROW-IN

In an elimination play, declarer's trumps threaten to make the defenders yield a ruff and sluff. However, declarer also can force the defenders to make a favorable lead at a no-trump contract.

```
                    NORTH
                    ♠ A K 4 3
                    ♡ 6 5
                    ◇ A Q 7 2
                    ♣ K 7 5
WEST                                    EAST
♠ J 10 9 8                              ♠ 7 6
♡ K 10 8 2                              ♡ J 9 7 4
◇ 6 5                                   ◇ J 10 9 8
♣ 9 8 3                                 ♣ J 10 6
                    SOUTH
                    ♠ Q 5 2
                    ♡ A Q 3
                    ◇ K 4 3
                    ♣ A Q 4 2
```

Contract· six no-trump by South
Opening lead· jack of spades

South wins the opening lead with the king and decides to
test each of his options in turn. He plays three rounds of
clubs and is pleased to see that suit split 3-3, giving him an
eleventh trick. He still needs one more. On the fourth round
of clubs, everyone discards a heart. South then cashes three
top diamonds, and West discards another heart. Next, declarer tries two more high spades—this time East discards a
second heart.

Declarer could finesse the heart queen now, but that is a
needless risk. West has a good spade and two hearts left, so
declarer exits with dummy's last spade and waits for West's
heart return.

AVOIDANCE

On some hands one defender will be ready and willing to do some damage, while the other defender will be harmless. Declarer's aim is to keep the dangerous defender from gaining the lead.

NORTH
♠ A J 9 4
♡ 9 3
♢ Q 10 3
♣ A Q 10 3

WEST
♠ 8 7 2
♡ A 10 8 5 2
♢ K 2
♣ 6 5 4

EAST
♠ K 6 5
♡ J 7 6
♢ 8 7 6 5
♣ 9 8 7

SOUTH
♠ Q 10 3
♡ K Q 4
♢ A J 9 4
♣ K J 2

Contract: three no-trump by South
Opening lead: five of hearts

East plays the jack on the first trick, and declarer's queen wins. Declarer has seven top tricks and easily can develop two more in spades or diamonds. He knows that West lurks with long hearts headed by the A-10 behind the king. If East gets in, a heart play through declarer will ruin him; if West wins a trick, however, declarer's king is safe from attack.

Taking all this into consideration, South should go to dummy with a club and take the *diamond* finesse. At worst this will lose to West, who can do no damage, and declarer now has nine tricks to take when he regains the lead. If instead declarer chose the *spade* finesse, he would be defeated when it lost to East.

HOLDUP

Change the heart suit in the last hand slightly.

                    NORTH
                    ♠ A J 9 4
                    ♡ 9 3
                    ◇ Q 10 3
                    ♣ A Q 10 3
WEST   EAST
♠ 8 7 2   ♠ K 6 5
♡ K 10 8 5 2   ♡ Q J 6
◇ K 2   ◇ 8 7 6 5
♣ 6 5 4   ♣ 9 8 7
                    SOUTH
                    ♠ Q 10 3
                    ♡ A 7 4
                    ◇ A J 9 4
                    ♣ K J 2

Contract: three no-trump by South
Opening lead: five of hearts

Declarer has only a single heart stopper, and he's about to lose it. All declarer can do is try to make it as hard as possible for the defenders to cash their good hearts if they win an early trick. To that end declarer *holds up* his heart ace twice, winning it on the third trick. As it happens, this exhausts East of hearts.

Declarer now takes the *spade* finesse. It loses, but East and West have no communication in the heart suit. East must give declarer back the lead to finish taking his nine tricks.

Notice that declarer combined his holdup with an *avoidance* play. This time, *West* was the dangerous opponent—he surely had good hearts to cash. So declarer chose to take a finesse which at worst would lose to *East*.

SETTING UP A SUIT (I)

Setting up a long suit at no-trump often means conceding a trick or two to the opposition. A *ducking* play is a simple way to preserve a vital entry while doing this.

NORTH
♠ A J
♡ J 5 3
♢ 10 7 4
♣ A 7 6 5 3

WEST
♠ Q 10 8 5 2
♡ 10 8 7 4
♢ 6 5
♣ K 4

EAST
♠ 7 6 4
♡ Q 9 6
♢ Q J 9 8
♣ Q 10 9

SOUTH
♠ K 9 3
♡ A K 2
♢ A K 3 2
♣ J 8 2

Contract: three no-trump by South
Opening lead: five of spades

Declarer puts in dummy's jack at trick one and is relieved when it holds the trick. He now has eight top tricks and has plenty of time to establish dummy's long clubs (assuming the likely 3-2 club break) for two more.

However, South must be careful not to release the club ace too soon. Suppose he mistakenly cashes the club ace at trick two and concedes a club to West's king. A second spade knocks out dummy's ace. Now declarer can give up another club to East's queen, setting up the long clubs, but he can't reach them—dummy has no further entry.

To save himself, declarer need only employ the *duck*, playing low clubs from both hands on the first two rounds of the suit. Then the third round can be won with dummy's ace, and declarer is in the right hand to cash the two club winners.

SETTING UP A SUIT (II)

In a trump contract declarer may be able to establish a side suit by trumping cards in the suit until it is good. This play often requires careful planning and close attention to entries.

NORTH
♠ K 3 2
♡ 4 3
◊ A 6 5 4 2
♣ K 4 3

WEST
♠ 9 8 4
♡ J 10 9 7 2
◊ J 10
♣ Q 10 8

EAST
♠ 5
♡ K 8 6 5
◊ K Q 9 8
♣ J 7 6 5

SOUTH
♠ A Q J 10 7 6
♡ A Q
◊ 7 3
♣ A 9 2

Contract: six spades by South
Opening lead: jack of hearts

The opening lead solves one of declarer's problems in this hand, but he still has a sure diamond loser and a possible club loser to contend with. Dummy's diamond suit is promising, and declarer should plan to establish it by trumping, obtaining a discard for his losing club. But if diamonds break 4-2 and that's the most likely division in this hand, three dummy entries will be needed—two to trump diamonds, the third to cash the long diamond.

The three entries are in the dummy all right—the diamond ace, spade king, and club king—but South must take care not to spend them too soon in the play of the hand. Obviously, all the trumps cannot be drawn first—just one trump can be drawn with the ace. Declarer then should lead a diamond and *duck* in dummy, saving the ace of diamonds entry until he is ready to start trumping.

Suppose East wins and returns a club. Declarer wins in hand, draws another trump with the queen, plays a diamond to the ace, and trumps a diamond with a high trump. A spade to the king draws the outstanding trump and another diamond is trumped, establishing the fifth diamond. The club king remains as an entry.

Unless declarer plays his cards in this precise order, the slam may fail.

FINDING ENTRIES

Being in the right place at the right time is at the heart of good declarer play. An observant declarer who studies the situation very carefully usually can unearth some way to place the lead where he wants it.

```
                        NORTH
                        ♠ Q J 9 2
                        ♡ 10 8 3
                        ◇ K 5 3 2
                        ♣ Q 6
        WEST                            EAST
        ♠ 8 7 6                         ♠ K 4 3
        ♡ K J 9 6 2                     ♡ Q 7 4
        ◇ 10 8 7                        ◇ 9 6
        ♣ A 3                           ♣ 9 8 7 5 4
                        SOUTH
                        ♠ A 10 5
                        ♡ A 5
                        ◇ A Q J 4
                        ♣ K J 10 2
```

173

Contract: three no-trump by South
Opening lead: six of hearts

South ducks East's queen at the first trick, but he has to win the heart continuation. Leading a club will allow West to win and cash out for down one, so declarer plans to make the contract with four tricks in spades.

Suppose South plays a low diamond to the king and finesses the spade queen and jack successfully. Now the spade ace drops East's king, but there is no fast entry to dummy to take the spade nine. Declarer must lead a club, and goes down. South, it seems, needs an extra entry to dummy. Can you spot it?

At trick three declarer should cash the diamond ace and queen and, when he sees that diamonds are splitting 3-2, *overtake* the jack with the king. After three rounds of spades have picked up the king, the diamond four is led to the five, and the fourth spade can be cashed.

MAKING THE MOST OF YOUR CHANCES

Sometimes declarer will have several chances for his contract. Good play will consist of trying all the possibilities in the proper order.

```
                    NORTH
                    ♠ Q632
                    ♡ 7642
                    ◇ Q7
                    ♣ A43
    WEST                          EAST
    ♠ K108                        ♠ 97
    ♡ 53                          ♡ J1098
    ◇ J10964                      ◇ K852
    ♣ 1087                        ♣ J96
                    SOUTH
                    ♠ AJ54
                    ♡ AKQ
                    ◇ A3
                    ♣ KQ52
```

Contract: three no-trump by South
Opening lead: jack of diamonds

Declarer tries the queen from dummy at trick one, but East's king covers, forcing the ace. Declarer has eight fast winners. The ninth can come from a winning spade finesse or from a 3-3 break in hearts or clubs. Since the defense can set the contract with diamonds if they get in, declarer should save the spade finesse as a last resort. First, he cashes the three top hearts. Nothing good happens there—West discards a spade on the third round. Next declarer tries the king, queen, and ace of clubs. When the even break shows up, declarer can play a spade to the *ace* and cash the fourth club for nine tricks.

If clubs had failed to break, declarer would want to be in dummy to try a spade to the jack. That's why it was best to cash the three high clubs *ending in dummy*.

KEEPING CONTROL OF TRUMPS

In a suit contract declarer's trumps buy him time to establish and cash other winners. If declarer's trump holding is tenuous or a bad break threatens, he must take care not to run out of trumps, thereby losing control of the play.

NORTH
♠ K 9 3
♡ Q 6 5
♢ 8 5 4 2
♣ K 3 2

WEST
♠ 10 8 7 6
♡ J 10 7 4
♢ K J 7
♣ 6 5

EAST
♠ 5 4
♡ A K 8 2
♢ Q 10 9 6
♣ 9 8 7

SOUTH
♠ A Q J 2
♡ 9 3
♢ A 3
♣ A Q J 10 4

Contract: four spades by South
Opening lead: jack of hearts

West's jack of hearts holds the first trick. East wins the second heart with the king and continues with the heart ace. Playing in a 4-3 fit, declarer faces control problems. If he trumps this trick, he will have lost control—West's long trump will score. Since declarer also has a diamond loser, the result will be down one.

Better play by South is to discard his small diamond on the third heart, a *loser-on-loser* play. This is a trick that must be lost in any event, and declarer keeps his trump holding intact.

Whatever the defenders lead next, declarer can win and draw all the trumps in four rounds, then cash his club tricks. (If the defenders lead a fourth round of hearts, declarer can ruff in *dummy*, saving the four-card trump length in his hand.)

CROSSRUFFING

On this deal, declarer uses his trumps one at a time by ruffing back and forth between his hand and the dummy.

```
                    NORTH
                    ♠ A J 9 7 6
                    ♡ A 5 4 3 2
                    ◇ 6
                    ♣ 8 5
    WEST                            EAST
    ♠ 5 4 3                         ♠ void
    ♡ J 9                           ♡ K Q 10 8 6
    ◇ K J 10 9 8 7                  ◇ Q
    ♣ 10 6                          ♣ Q J 9 7 4 3 2
                    SOUTH
                    ♠ K Q 10 8 2
                    ♡ 7
                    ◇ A 5 4 3 2
                    ♣ A K
```

Contract: seven spades by South
Opening lead: ten of clubs

South wins the first club and takes stock. He has no apparent losers, but his problem is to find thirteen winners. He counts one trick in each red suit, plus two in clubs. He needs nine tricks in the trump suit, and he can take them on a crossruff.

He can afford one trump lead if he can score the remaining eight trumps separately, so he leads the two of trumps and wins in dummy. Next, he cashes the red aces and the other high club. At this point he can show his hand—his other trumps are all high, and nothing can interfere with the crossruff.

In this kind of play declarer must take care to cash all his side winners before he starts to crossruff. If South fails to take both high clubs before crossruffing on this deal, West will discard a club somewhere along the line and the hand will be set.

DUMMY REVERSAL

Declarer usually has the greater trump length in his hand and uses it to draw trumps. In a *dummy reversal*, he manufactures an extra trick by ruffing several cards in his hand and eventually drawing trumps with dummy's trumps.

NORTH
♠ K 10 8
♡ Q 7 5 3
◇ A 5 4
♣ A K 3

WEST
♠ 7 6 5
♡ J 10 8 6
◇ Q 10 6
♣ 7 6 5

EAST
♠ 4 2
♡ A K 9 4
◇ J 9 8 7
♣ 10 9 8

SOUTH
♠ A Q J 9 3
♡ 2
◇ K 3 2
♣ Q J 4 2

Contract: six spades by South
Opening lead: jack of hearts

Suppose West wins the first trick and shifts to a diamond. Declarer wins in hand with the king and tests trumps by playing the ace and king. When he sees the 3-2 break, he can continue with a heart ruff, a diamond to the ace and another heart ruff. A club to the king allows declarer to ruff dummy's last heart with his last trump. Dummy is entered with the club ace and the last trump is drawn, with declarer discarding a diamond from his hand. The queen and jack of clubs win the last two tricks.

A typical dummy reversal has two requirements. First, dummy must have extra-good trumps and plenty of entries. Second, trumps must divide favorably so declarer can draw trumps with the shorter trumps in dummy. (If declarer found the trumps split 4-1 on the deal above, he'd have to abandon the dummy reversal and play clubs, hoping the hand with four trumps also had four clubs. He could then discard a diamond from dummy and trump his diamond loser.)

GOOD TIMING

The play in a no-trump contract amounts to a race between declarer and the defense to see who can establish their tricks first. While the defenders enjoy the advantage of making the opening lead, declarer can take precautions if he sees that he might lose the race.

```
                    NORTH
                    ♠ J 3
                    ♡ 6 5 4
                    ◇ A J 9 5 3
                    ♣ K Q 3
        WEST                        EAST
        ♠ 10 9 8 7 6                ♠ Q 5 4
        ♡ J 9 7                     ♡ Q 10 8 2
        ◇ 6 2                       ◇ K 8 7
        ♣ A 10 2                    ♣ J 9 8
                    SOUTH
                    ♠ A K 2
                    ♡ A K 3
                    ◇ Q 10 4
                    ♣ 7 6 5 4
```

Contract: three no-trump by South
Opening lead: ten of spades

Declarer hopefully put up dummy's jack on the opening lead, but East's queen drove out the ace. A diamond finesse lost to the king, and a spade came back. Declarer held up his ace and won the third spade. Since he had only eight tricks, he had to lead a club. West pounced with his ace and cashed two more spades to set the contract one trick.

Declarer should have figured that the contract was in danger only if West, who undoubtedly had the long spades, won a trick *after his suit was good.* Since West's only possible entry was the ace of clubs, that card should have been dislodged first.

At trick two South should lead a club. If the king wins in dummy, he switches to diamonds. But suppose somebody wins the club ace and returns a spade. Declarer holds off, takes the third spade, and tries the diamond finesse. If East can win the king, he probably will have no spades left. (If he does have one, the suit has split 4-4 and declarer loses only four tricks in all.)

WATCHING OUT FOR BLOCKED SUITS

Maintaining concentration and paying close attention to detail are the marks of a fine declarer. Just knowing the techniques of good play won't help if you lack the presence of mind to apply them.

NORTH
♠ J 7
♡ 10 6 4
◇ A K Q 4 2
♣ 5 4 3

WEST
♠ K 10 8 5 3
♡ 9 7
◇ J 9 5
♣ A J 9

EAST
♠ Q 6 4
♡ J 8 5 3 2
◇ 10
♣ Q 10 8 6

SOUTH
♠ A 9 2
♡ A K Q
◇ 8 7 6 3
♣ K 7 2

Contract: three no-trump by South
Opening lead: five of spades

Declarer correctly put up dummy's jack at trick one—this was the only chance to win two spade tricks. When East's queen came up, declarer won the ace immediately. He could see nine tricks, barring a terrible diamond division, and he wasn't anxious for East to shift to a club through the king.

When declarer then turned his attention to the diamonds, he did not make the error of leading the two from his hand. Instead, he got one of his higher spots out of the way—under the diamond ace, king, and queen he dumped the eight, seven, and six. On the fourth round of the suit the four outranked the three, and the lead stayed in dummy so the two could be cashed for the all-important ninth trick.

DECEPTION

There are plenty of chances to pull the wool over your opponents' eyes at the bridge table. One technique that can prove startlingly effective is *winning a trick with a higher card than necessary*.

NORTH
♠ 8 6 2
♡ 8 7
◇ Q J 8 7
♣ A Q 6 5

WEST
♠ K J 9 3
♡ K 10 6 4 2
◇ K 3
♣ 8 2

EAST
♠ A 10 7 4
♡ J 9 5
◇ 6 4
♣ 10 9 4 3

SOUTH
♠ Q 5
♡ A Q 3
◇ A 10 9 5 2
♣ K J 7

Contract: three no-trump by South
Opening lead: four of hearts

When this hand was played in a team-of-four match, the contract and the opening lead were the same at both tables.

At the first table declarer took East's jack of hearts with the queen, went to dummy with a club and tried the diamond finesse. West won the king and could see that the contract was impregnable if South held the ace of spades. So West shifted to a low spade. East won and returned the suit, and declarer had to go down one.

When the hand was replayed, South gave himself an extra chance in case the diamond king was wrong—he won the first trick with the *ace* of hearts!

West naturally thought his opening lead had struck gold. When the diamond finesse lost to the king, he continued with a second low heart. Great was his dismay when South produced the queen and claimed ten tricks.

COUNTING

A winning declarer tries to find out how many cards his opponents hold in each suit. This is a matter of checking the cards they play against the 13 they were dealt originally.

NORTH
♠ A K 6
♡ K J 10 9
♢ A 10 3
♣ 4 3 2

WEST
♠ 9 7 5
♡ 6 3
♢ 4
♣ Q J 10 9 8 7 6

EAST
♠ 10 4 3 2
♡ 7 2
♢ Q 8 7 6 5 2
♣ 5

SOUTH
♠ Q J 8
♡ A Q 8 5 4
♢ K J 9
♣ A K

Contract: seven no-trump by South
Opening lead: queen of clubs

South has twelve top tricks and a two-way finesse for the queen of diamonds for his thirteenth. It usually will pay him to postpone the crucial diamond guess until he plays out the other suits and gets some useful information.

As the cards lie, declarer can transform his two-way guess into a sure thing simply by cashing all his high cards outside diamonds. East will show out on the second club lead, so South will know that West started with seven clubs. West will follow to three spades and two hearts, so twelve of West's cards will be known. West cannot hold more than one diamond.

A diamond lead to dummy's ace will produce the four from West. With West out of diamonds a second-round finesse against East is sure to work.

DRAWING AN INFERENCE

Counting distribution is just one way to locate a missing queen. On page 161, we saw how declarer guessed a two-way finesse based on a clue from the bidding. On the deal below, declarer's clue comes from the way the defenders have played.

```
Dlr: East          NORTH
Vul: N-S           ♠ Q 7 6 3
                   ♡ K 5
                   ◇ Q 7 6
                   ♣ K 10 3 2

WEST                              EAST
♠ 9 5                            ♠ A 8
♡ 10 8 6 4                       ♡ A Q J 9 3
◇ J 9 8 5 4                      ◇ K 10 3 2
♣ Q 8                            ♣ 9 6

                   SOUTH
                   ♠ K J 10 4 2
                   ♡ 7 2
                   ◇ A
                   ♣ A J 7 5 4
```

WEST	NORTH	EAST	SOUTH
		1H	1S
Pass	2S	Pass	4S
All Pass			

South's bidding was a little optimistic, but the contract was a more than reasonable one. West led a heart, and East took the ace and jack. Next, East cashed the spade ace and exited with a spade lead, leaving the declarer to work out the clubs for himself.

Declarer played to the king of clubs and led a second club from dummy. When East followed low, declarer paused to consider the situation. He was tempted to try a finesse for the jack of clubs, playing East for the queen because he had opened the bidding. But when he made a recount it indicated that East could have had an opening bid without the club queen—holding the diamond king, plus the top hearts and spade ace, would have been enough.

With a count of the opponents' high-card points inconclusive, declarer decided to rely on an inference from the opening lead. If West had held a singleton club, he might well have led it, especially when he knew his partner had a good hand. (In fact, the contract always could have been beaten if West had a singleton club.)

When declarer put up the club ace, he was justly rewarded and made the contract.

SAFETY PLAY (I)

A safety play is intended to give you the best chance to take a desired number of tricks in a suit rather than the greatest number of tricks. It may not be as dramatic but it will bring in the contract.

```
                    NORTH
                    ♠ A 8 6 4
                    ♡ 7 5 4
                    ◇ A K Q J 7
                    ♣ 8
    WEST                            EAST
    ♠ Q 10 5 3                      ♠ void
    ♡ K J 9 6 2                     ♡ Q 10 8 3
    ◇ 9 6                           ◇ 8 5 2
    ♣ 10 9                          ♣ J 7 5 4 3 2
                    SOUTH
                    ♠ K J 9 7 2
                    ♡ A
                    ◇ 10 4 3
                    ♣ A K Q 6
```

Contract: six spades by South
Opening lead: ten of clubs

You can afford to lose one spade trick and still make the slam, but not two. If the suit breaks 2-2 or 3-1, there will be no worries—only a 4-0 break can endanger the contract. A careless declarer would start by leading a low trump to dummy's ace. East would show out, and West would take two trump tricks.

An expert starts by cashing the trump king, a play that guarantees the slam against any lie of the missing spades. When East shows out, South leads another trump and wins the trick as cheaply as possible in dummy. Whatever West does, he will be held to one trump trick.

Should *West* show out on the first round of trumps, South leads to dummy's ace and continues the suit, leading toward the jack. This time East can take no more than one trump trick.

SAFETY PLAY (II)

Some safety plays may wind up gaining a trick for you as against normal play. The following hand was played by Oswald Jacoby in the forties.

NORTH
♠ K Q 6 5
♡ 9 7 4
♦ 6 2
♣ A Q 5 4

WEST
♠ J 10 9 4
♡ K
♦ 10 9 7 3
♣ 10 8 6 2

EAST
♠ A 8 7 3
♡ J 6 5
♦ 8 5 4
♣ J 9 7

SOUTH
♠ 2
♡ A Q 10 8 3 2
♦ A K Q J
♣ K 3

Contract: six hearts
Opening lead: jack of spades

East won the first trick with the ace of spades and returned a diamond. Playing at six, Jacoby took the best play for the contract, a finesse of the heart queen. This lost to the singleton king. When Jacoby played the ace of hearts next, he wound up going down two tricks.

Had Jacoby been at a more conservative five-heart contract, he would have used the standard safety play of laying down the ace of hearts first. As it happened, this would have dropped the singleton king, whereupon he would have gone to dummy, finessed against the jack and made six. Had West and East both followed with small hearts on the first lead,

Jacoby would have gone to dummy and led toward the trump queen.

This safety play holds the trump loss to one trick unless West has K-J-x or K-J-x-x. In both of these cases there is no way to avoid losing two trump tricks.

PERCENTAGE PLAY

To solve some declarer-play problems, you must rely strictly on mathematics—there will be nothing else to fall back on. Luckily, an elementary knowledge of percentages is often enough to steer you right.

NORTH
♠ 8 7
♡ 3 2
◇ 8 7 6
♣ A K 5 4 3 2

WEST
♠ Q 6 5 4
♡ 9 8 7 6
◇ 5
♣ Q 1 0 9 8

EAST
♠ K 9 3 2
♡ J 1 0 5 4
◇ 9 4 3 2
♣ J

SOUTH
♠ A J 1 0
♡ A K Q
◇ A K Q J 1 0
♣ 7 6

Contract: six no-trump by South
Opening lead: nine of hearts

Declarer has two possible lines of play. Line (1) is to duck the first round of clubs, banking on a 3-2 break. Line (2) is to use the ace and king of clubs as entries to double-finesse in spades. Declarer must commit himself to one line or the other immediately, and there are no clues from the bidding or play and no psychological considerations.

In fact, the double finesse in spades is about a three-to-one favorite to produce the twelfth trick, while a 3-2 club break will happen only about 68% of the time. That makes the spade play a strong favorite in the percentage sweepstakes.

SQUEEZE

In a *squeeze* declarer forces the opponents to let him take a trick with a low card by making it impossible for them to guard against it.

                    NORTH
                    ♠ A J 9 2
                    ♡ A J 3
                    ◇ 7 5 4
                    ♣ A 4 3
WEST   EAST
♠ K Q 10 6 5 4   ♠ 8 7
♡ 7   ♡ 9
◇ A Q 9 8   ◇ 10 6 3 2
♣ K 10   ♣ J 9 8 6 5 2
                    SOUTH
                    ♠ 3
                    ♡ K Q 10 8 6 5 4 2
                    ◇ K J
                    ♣ Q 7

Contract: four hearts by South
Opening lead: king of spades

There is no problem making four hearts—South has ten of the easiest tricks ever seen. But he might as well make eleven. (In tournament bridge an overtrick in this normal contract would be needed for a good score.)

South wins the opening lead in dummy, plays one trump, and then leads a diamond from dummy. With West holding both the ace and queen, it doesn't matter which diamond South plays. West wins, cashes a second diamond and leads a third diamond, which South trumps.

Now South simply runs all his trumps, and the last one squeezes West. Here's how the ending looks:

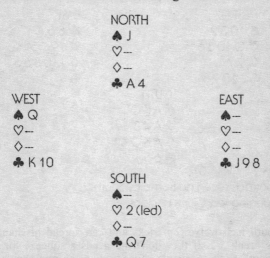

```
                    NORTH
                    ♠ J
                    ♡ —
                    ◇ —
                    ♣ A 4
   WEST                              EAST
   ♠ Q                               ♠ —
   ♡ —                               ♡ —
   ◇ —                               ◇ —
   ♣ K 10                            ♣ J 9 8
                    SOUTH
                    ♠ —
                    ♡ 2 (led)
                    ◇ —
                    ♣ Q 7
```

If West unguards the king of clubs to save the queen of spades, the jack of spades is thrown from dummy and the ace and queen of clubs take the last two tricks. If West discards the spade queen, dummy throws the small club and takes the last two tricks with the ace of clubs and the jack of spades.

DOUBLE SQUEEZE

In this play declarer squeezes *both* opponents in turn. Declarer has "threat cards" in three suits. In the end one defender has to guard suit A, the other defender must guard suit B, so neither defender can hang on to suit C. In many types of double squeezes declarer must cash his winners in precisely the right order.

```
                    NORTH
                    ♠ 9 7 6
                    ♡ K 2
                    ◇ 3 2
                    ♣ A K Q 4 3 2
WEST                                    EAST
♠ 1 0 3 2                               ♠ 8 5 4
♡ Q 1 0 8 6                             ♡ J 9 7 5
◇ 9 7                                   ◇ J 1 0 8 6 5
♣ J 1 0 9 8                             ♣ 7
                    SOUTH
                    ♠ A K Q J
                    ♡ A 4 3
                    ◇ A K Q 4
                    ♣ 6 5
```

Contract: seven no-trump by South
Opening lead: jack of clubs

South has twelve top tricks and can spread his hand if clubs break 3-2. If they don't, he needs a squeeze for the thirteenth trick. A simple squeeze (like the one shown on page 190) will operate easily if the same defender holds four clubs and four diamonds. In this case, however, West has clubs stopped while East has diamonds stopped. Nevertheless, because South has three hearts, he can use the third heart as an extra threat.

He begins by cashing a second club and finds out about the bad break in that suit. He must not take a third club now because he would have to discard a vital heart or diamond from his hand. Instead, he runs off four spades, discarding a club from dummy. By this time, East has discarded twice, throwing a diamond and a heart. West has let a heart go. Both defenders still have hearts protected.

Now South cashes three high diamonds, and West is squeezed—he has to throw away another heart and no longer can protect that suit. Another club is thrown from dummy.

A heart to dummy's king followed by the last high club puts the squeeze on East, who has to throw away another heart to keep the high diamond. South discards the four of diamonds and takes the last two tricks with the heart ace and a small heart.

This double squeeze is called *nonsimultaneous* because each defender is squeezed on a different trick.

LOOK-ALIKES

One of the great difficulties of dummy play is that many card combinations look alike but call for very different lines of play. Here are a few examples. In each case you want to play the single suit shown to best advantage. It is assumed you have enough entries to lead from either hand as often as necessary.

DIAGRAM A   DIAGRAM B
K J 9 2   K J 6 2
A 10   A 10

In both these cases three tricks are certain, provided you do nothing ridiculous. Which line of play will give you the best chance for four tricks?

With A the best play is to cash the ace, continue with the 10, and finesse if West plays low. This will produce four tricks if either player holds a singleton queen, or if West started with the queen plus one or two small cards.

With B dummy lacks the nine. If you play the same way and West has the queen, he will cover the 10 and you will be held to three tricks. It is correct to play East for the queen, leading low to the 10. You will lose to the singleton queen in the West hand, but you take four tricks any time East started with a singleton, doubleton, or tripleton queen.

DIAGRAM A	DIAGRAM B
A 10	5 4
K Q 5 4 3	A K Q 10 3

You need five tricks in the suit. With A you lead toward dummy and finesse the 10. You take five tricks whenever West has J-x, J-x-x or J-x-x-x, almost a 50% chance. If you play out the top cards, you take five tricks if the suit breaks 3-3 (about one chance in three).

With B it is slightly better to play off the top honors. You take five tricks any time the suit breaks 3-3, or when either defender has J-x.

DIAGRAM A	DIAGRAM B
9 7 2	9 2
A K J 10 8	A K J 10 8 7

With A the best play is to cash the ace, then go to dummy and finesse. You take all the tricks if there is a singleton queen on either side, or if East has two, three, or four to the queen. You lose a trick if the suit breaks 5-0, or if West started with the queen and at least one small card.

With B take a *first-round* finesse. If you play a high card first, you take care of a singleton queen with West. But you lose a trick you could have won if West's singleton is one of the four low cards.

This time dummy is void. You hold:

A. A Q 10 9 8 7 6
B. A Q 9 8 7 6 5
C. A Q 6 5 4 3 2

With all three holdings you start by playing out the ace. With A you continue with the queen. You can hold your losses to just one trick if either defender has the doubleton jack.

With B it is easy to see that you should continue with the queen if the jack or ten drops on the first round. You also should continue with the queen if both defenders follow with low cards on the ace. If the remaining four cards break 2-2, all plays lose two tricks. The queen-play loses a trick if the king is now bare, but it gains a trick if jack or ten drops (twice as likely).

With C you lead a low card on the second round. This saves a trick if either opponent started with K-x. Nothing helps you against any other 4-2 break.

DIAGRAM A   DIAGRAM B
K Q 9 6 4   K Q 9 6 4
A 10 3 2   A 5 3 2

In A be sure to cash the king or queen first. In case of a 4-0 break you still will have a finessing position against either defender to pick up the whole suit.

In B cash the ace first. If East shows out, you still can take five tricks by finessing twice through West. If West is void, you must lose a trick however you play.

DIAGRAM A   DIAGRAM B
K 4 3   K 4 3 2
A J 6 5   A J 6 5

If you need four tricks in the suit, the correct play with either holding is to cash dummy's king, then lead toward your hand and finesse the jack.

If you need just three tricks, this is also the correct play with B. With A you should take the ace and king, then lead toward the jack. You win three tricks any time East holds the queen, or West has the doubleton queen. Of course, this approach gives up any chance for four tricks.

In the next situation, we are concerned with only one combination:

Q 4 3 2
K 7 6 5

Suppose you start by leading toward dummy. Say West plays low and the queen holds. Now you lead back toward your own hand and play *low*. This is known as an *obligatory finesse*. You can't gain by playing the king—you know West's ace will capture it—so you are obligated to play low. You are hoping West started with A-x, in which case he *must* play the ace, making your king good.

Is there any difference between playing this way and starting by leading toward your king? No, but a good player makes neither play blindly. If he thinks West holds the ace, he makes the first lead toward dummy; if he thinks East holds the ace, he starts by leading toward his hand.

If he has no idea where the ace is, he decides which opponent is more likely to have only two cards in the suit. The obligatory finesse works only against a doubleton ace, so declarer makes the first lead through the hand with the presumed doubleton.

Here are some other single-suit combinations and the ways to play them for the maximum number of tricks:

1. J 6 5 4 2
   A Q 9 8 3

Finesse for the king. Be sure to lead the jack first, saving a trick if East has K-10-7.

2. A 6 5 3
   Q 10 9 8

Try a double finesse. Lead the eight and play low from dummy. If it loses to the jack, lead the nine next and play low from dummy again.

3. A 10 4
   Q 5 3

Lead low to the queen. If that loses to the king, lead low to the ten next.

4. A J 9
   4 3 2

Lead low to the nine. Assuming you lose to the king or queen, lead low to the jack next. This is the best play for two tricks, winning if West has the ten plus one other honor—this will happen three times in eight.

5. A Q 9
   4 3 2

If you need two tricks and have plenty of time to get them, finesse the nine first. If West holds both the jack and ten, the nine will drive out the king. If the nine loses to the jack or ten, finesse the queen next.

6. A
   J 10 5 4 3 2

Cash the ace, come back to hand, and lead a low card. If the defenders' cards are divided 3-3, your play is immaterial. Leading low the second time gains if someone has a doubleton king or queen.

7. J 10 5 4
   A 9 8 3 2

A double finesse is the best play, but not by much.

8. A K 9 3
   J 4 3 2

Your best play for four tricks is to cash the ace and king, hoping the queen will drop. However, if you want to ensure three tricks, cash the ace and lead low toward the jack.

Defensive Play

SECOND-HAND PLAY

The tendency by second hand to play low applies for the defenders as well as declarer. In this position

$$654$$

$$J732 \qquad\qquad\qquad A109$$

$$KQ8$$

declarer leads low from dummy. If East plays low, declarer wins with the king or queen. But now he must find some way to return to dummy to lead toward his remaining honor. By playing *second hand low* East can make declarer's task just a little tougher.

Second hand low usually is a reliable dictum, but there are plenty of times when it is better ignored.

```
                    NORTH
                    ♠ K 6
                    ♡ J 9 6 3
                    ◇ K Q 5 3
                    ♣ K 6 5
  WEST                              EAST
  ♠ Q J 1 0 8 5                     ♠ 9 7 4
  ♡ 1 0 8 5                         ♡ A 7 4
  ◇ A 2                             ◇ 8 7 6
  ♣ 7 4 3                           ♣ J 1 0 9 8
                    SOUTH
                    ♠ A 3 2
                    ♡ K Q 2
                    ◇ J 1 0 9 4
                    ♣ A Q 2
```

Contract: three no-trump by South
Opening lead: queen of spades

Declarer wins the first trick with dummy's king and immediately leads a low heart. East should *go right up with the ace*
to return a spade. The idea is for East to establish partner's
long suit while West still has *his* entry. So East should be
anxious to win an early trick even if it means ignoring *second
hand low*.

If declarer is allowed to steal a heart trick, he will switch to
diamonds for nine tricks.

COVERING HONORS

A special case in second-hand play arises when declarer leads a high card. A defender may gain by covering with a high card of his own, forcing declarer to spend *two* high cards to win the trick.

```
                          J 6
      8 5 4 2                            K 9 3
                        A Q 10 7
```

The jack is led from dummy. If East plays low, declarer finesses, repeats the finesse and takes four tricks. But if East covers the jack with the king, West's eight will control the fourth round of the suit.

However, it's silly to blithely cover every honor declarer leads.

```
                    NORTH
                    ♠ J 4
                    ♡ K 6 5
                    ◊ A K 6 5 3
                    ♣ 6 4 3
      WEST                            EAST
      ♠ 8 3                           ♠ Q 5 2
      ♡ J 10 7                        ♡ Q 9 8 2
      ◊ J 9 7 2                       ◊ 10 8 4
      ♣ K J 7 2                       ♣ A 10 9
                    SOUTH
                    ♠ A K 10 9 7 6
                    ♡ A 4 3
                    ◊ Q
                    ♣ Q 8 5
```

WEST	NORTH	EAST	SOUTH
			1S
Pass	2D	Pass	2S
Pass	3S	Pass	4S
All Pass			

West leads a low club, and the defenders take the first three tricks. Declarer wins a heart shift in dummy and calls for the jack of spades. East should play low without hesitation. The bidding marks declarer with length and strength in spades, so nothing can be gained by covering.

THIRD-HAND PLAY

One of the often-repeated defensive "rules" is for third hand to play high.

864

Q1052   K93

AJ7

West leads the two of this suit. East should willingly sacrifice his king, hoping to promote the intermediate cards in West's hand.

Like most of the other rules, this one has many exceptions. On this deal East has to avoid playing *third hand high* to keep the defenders' lines of communication open.

```
                        NORTH
                        ♠ 8 4
                        ♡ 9 7 3
                        ◇ K Q 10
                        ♣ A J 10 8 7
        WEST                                EAST
        ♠ J 9 7 5 2                         ♠ A Q 6
        ♡ Q J 4                             ♡ 8 6 5
        ◇ 8 4                               ◇ J 7 6 3 2
        ♣ 6 5 3                             ♣ K 4
                        SOUTH
                        ♠ K 10 3
                        ♡ A K 10 2
                        ◇ A 9 5
                        ♣ Q 9 2
```

Contract: three no-trump by South
Opening lead: five of spades

If East clatters up with the ace of spades on the opening
lead, South will make ten tricks. South will duck East's lead
of the spade queen at trick two and win the third spade. The
club finesse will lose to East, but he will have no way to put
his partner in the lead. South will take the rest of the tricks.

East's correct play at trick one is the *queen* of spades.
South can still make the hand if he holds off the king, but he
isn't looking at the opponents' cards. He really would look
silly if it turned out that West had led from the A-J of spades.
Therefore, South surely will go right up with the king and
hope the club finesse will work. When it loses, East cashes
the ace of spades and leads his last spade to partner to set the
contract.

RULE OF ELEVEN

The Rule of Eleven is a handy device that can make third-hand play easier. Subtract from eleven the spot that partner led. If you assume his lead is fourth-best, the remainder equals the number of higher cards held by you, declarer, and dummy.

NORTH
♠ K J 10 6 4
♡ K 6 4
◇ A 3
♣ 8 5 3

WEST
♠ 7 5 3
♡ Q 10 8 7
◇ J 9 2
♣ J 9 4

EAST
♠ A 9
♡ A J 9 3
◇ 10 7 5 4
♣ 7 6 2

SOUTH
♠ Q 8 2
♡ 5 2
◇ K Q 8 6
♣ A K Q 10

Contract: three no-trump by South
Opening lead: seven of hearts

The key play comes at trick one, when declarer follows with a low heart from dummy. To determine the winning play, East can use the *Rule of Eleven*. He subtracts seven, the spot that West led, from eleven. The remainder is four. So among the dummy, East, and declarer, there are four hearts higher than the seven.

Since East can see all four of those hearts in his own hand and dummy, he knows that *declarer cannot beat West's lead.*

East can safely play the three, allowing partner to hold the trick. West can lead through dummy's king again, and the defenders will wind up with four heart tricks and the ace of spades.

If East played any other heart at trick one, South would make his game.

WHEN TO GET BUSY

On most hands, the defenders have a major decision to make. Should they search aggressively for tricks in a big hurry? Or should they sit back, let declarer spin his wheels, and wait for tricks to fall into their laps? To answer this question, they must judge the strengths and weaknesses of dummy.

```
                    NORTH
                    ♠ Q 10 3
                    ♡ 3
                    ◇ A 10 4 3
                    ♣ K Q J 10 7
    WEST                              EAST
    ♠ 8 7                             ♠ 4 2
    ♡ Q 10 6 2                        ♡ A 9 8 5 4
    ◇ Q 9 5                           ◇ K J 6
    ♣ A 9 6 5                         ♣ 8 4 2
                    SOUTH
                    ♠ A K J 9 6 5
                    ♡ K J 7
                    ◇ 8 7 2
                    ♣ 3
```

WEST	NORTH	EAST	SOUTH
			1S
Pass	2C	Pass	2S
Pass	4S	All Pass	

West leads the two of hearts to East's ace, and the crucial point of the hand is reached. East can see that dummy is very strong. The club suit will provide plenty of tricks, and declarer, given time, surely will establish it and throw away his losing diamonds.

To give the defense a chance, East must fearlessly lead a diamond away from the K-J at the second trick, playing West for the diamond queen as well as the club ace or a trick in trumps. There is no time to lose! If declarer turns up with the queen of diamonds, East's play will have cost nothing—declarer would have discarded his diamonds on the clubs anyway.

This is an *active* defense by East, a desperate attempt to set up and cash tricks before it is too late.

WHEN TO GO PASSIVE

When dummy is weak in high cards and has no threatening long suit, the defenders' approach changes from aggressive to passive. Now declarer will have no way to get rid of his losers, so the defenders need only play safe and wait for declarer to go down. Snatching aces, leading away from honors, and breaking new suits are all unnecessary . . . and can be costly.

```
                    NORTH
                    ♠ A K 5 4
                    ♡ 10 9
                    ◇ 8 7 6 5
                    ♣ 8 7 6
    WEST                            EAST
    ♠ J 10 9 8                      ♠ Q 7 6 2
    ♡ 7 6                           ♡ J 8 5
    ◇ Q 4 3                         ◇ K 9 2
    ♣ A J 5 2                       ♣ Q 10 9
                    SOUTH
                    ♠ 3
                    ♡ A K Q 4 3 2
                    ◇ A J 10
                    ♣ K 4 3
```

Contract: four hearts by South
Opening lead: jack of spades

South wins the spade ace and continues with the king, discarding a club. He then elects to finesse the jack of diamonds, West winning the queen.

At this point dummy is no longer a factor. There is nothing there declarer can use to avoid any of his losers. So West should be content to get out of the lead safely and let declarer struggle. West's safest exit is a spade, forcing declarer to ruff. After this, declarer must lose another diamond and two clubs for down one.

If West led back any other suit, the contract probably would be made.

THE FORCING DEFENSE

If the defenders can make declarer use up all his trumps, *control* of the hand will pass over to them. A ruff and sluff usually is viewed as a defensive cardinal sin, but on this hand the defenders can attack declarer's trump holding by giving him repeated ruff-sluffs.

NORTH
♠ Q J 9 3
♡ 7 3
◇ A 8 5 3
♣ K 6 5

WEST
♠ A 8 7 6
♡ K J 9 4 2
◇ J 2
♣ 4 3

EAST
♠ 5
♡ A 10 8 6
◇ 10 9 7 6
♣ 10 9 8 7

SOUTH
♠ K 10 4 2
♡ Q 5
◇ K Q 4
♣ A Q J 2

WEST	NORTH	EAST	SOUTH
			1NT
Pass	2C	Pass	2S
Pass	4S	All Pass	

West knows that North and South are playing in a 4-4 fit. His four trumps could give declarer some problems, especially if declarer can be forced to ruff a couple of times. The suit that declarer is most likely to have to ruff is West's longest, so West chooses the heart four as his opening lead. East wins the ace and returns a heart to the queen and king.

Now West can tell that there are no more side-suit tricks available to the defense. If declarer has 16 high-card points for his one no-trump opening, East holds at most only another jack. An extra trump trick is the only chance for the defense, so West continues with a third heart. True, this gives declarer a ruff-sluff, but it doesn't help him because he has only winning cards to sluff.

Suppose declarer ruffs in dummy and leads the queen of spades. If West wins this trick, declarer is safe—he can ruff a fourth heart lead in dummy again, saving the trumps in his hand to draw trumps with.

Instead, West should hold up his spade ace and hold up again if declarer continues with the spade jack. Now declarer's goose is cooked. If he leads still another trump, West wins and plays another heart. Since dummy is now out of trumps, declarer must ruff in his hand with his last trump, and West has gained control.

SURPRISE TRUMP TRICKS ON DEFENSE

When all appears lost, the defenders still may be able to invent some tricks . . . in declarer's best suit!

There are two possibilities. In a *trump promotion*, declarer is placed in a position where he can (1) ruff low and be overruffed or (2) ruff high, setting up a natural trump trick for the defender who sits behind him.

76

K94   103

AQJ852

This suit is trumps, and East leads a side suit of which both declarer and West are void. If declarer ruffs low, West overruffs with the nine and later takes the king for two tricks. If declarer ruffs with the queen, West has to be careful—to come to two tricks, he must *discard* rather than overruff immediately with the king.

In the *uppercut*, one defender ruffs in with a fairly high trump. This sets up a trump trick for his partner when declarer has to spend a higher trump to overruff.

NORTH
♠ 8 4 2
♡ J 7 4 2
◇ K Q J 7
♣ A 2

WEST
♠ A K Q J 9 5
♡ Q 3
◇ 8 6
♣ K J 9

EAST
♠ 10 3
♡ 10
◇ 10 5 4 3 2
♣ Q 10 7 6 5

SOUTH
♠ 7 6
♡ A K 9 8 6 5
◇ A 9
♣ 8 4 3

Contract: five hearts by South
Opening lead: ace of spades

South opened the bidding with one heart, and East-West pushed him up to five. West cashes two spade tricks and decides that the only way to beat the hand is to find partner with the ten of hearts. To make sure partner ruffs in, West continues with a *low* spade. Sure enough, East is able to trump with the ten. This forces South to use one of his high trumps, and West's queen is established as the setting trick.

KILLING DUMMY

An alternative defense at no-trump is keeping declarer from using his best suit. The way to do this is to ruin his lines of communication.

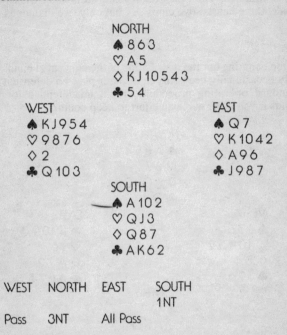

```
                    NORTH
                    ♠ 8 6 3
                    ♡ A 5
                    ◇ K J 10 5 4 3
                    ♣ 5 4
    WEST                              EAST
    ♠ K J 9 5 4                       ♠ Q 7
    ♡ 9 8 7 6                         ♡ K 10 4 2
    ◇ 2                               ◇ A 9 6
    ♣ Q 10 3                          ♣ J 9 8 7
                    SOUTH
                  ─ ♠ A 10 2
                    ♡ Q J 3
                    ◇ Q 8 7
                    ♣ A K 6 2
```

WEST	NORTH	EAST	SOUTH
			1NT
Pass	3NT	All Pass	

West leads the five of spades, East plays the queen, and declarer must hold up the ace. Before mechanically returning partner's lead, East should think things over. On the bidding there aren't enough missing high-card points for West to have an establishable spade suit plus a fast entry. So East temporarily should forget about setting up West's spades and concentrate on more pressing matters—eliminating dummy's diamond suit. If declarer can be prevented from using those diamonds, the contract surely will fail.

Taking no chances, East shifts to the *king* of hearts to dislodge dummy's ace. (If declarer refuses to win this, a second heart lead knocks out the ace.) When declarer attacks diamonds, East holds up the ace twice, leaving dummy's long cards stranded. The best declarer can do is eight tricks—a spade, three hearts, two clubs . . . but only two diamonds.

COUNTING

While counting out the distribution of the concealed hands is only occasionally necessary in declarer play, on defense it is standard operating procedure. You'll misdefend a lot of hands if you don't make an effort to keep count.

```
                    NORTH
                    ♠ A 8 5 4 2
                    ♡ 8 7
                    ◊ K Q 10 3
                    ♣ Q 4
      WEST                           EAST
      ♠ J 7 6                        ♠ K 10 9 3
      ♡ 10 9 5 2                     ♡ J 6
      ◊ 8 4                          ◊ A 7 2
      ♣ J 9 6 2                      ♣ A 8 7 5
                    SOUTH
                    ♠ Q
                    ♡ A K Q 4 3
                    ◊ J 9 6 5
                    ♣ K 10 3
```

WEST	NORTH	EAST	SOUTH
			1H
Pass	1S	Pass	2D
Pass	3D	Pass	3NT
All Pass			

West leads the two of clubs, and East takes his ace when dummy plays low. If East returns a club, declarer wins, knocks out the ace of diamonds, wins the next club, and runs for home with nine tricks—three hearts, three diamonds, two clubs, and a spade.

In this hand, the killing return by East at trick two is the *king of spades*—this return sets up three spade tricks to go along with the defenders' two aces. Can East figure out this play? Let's take a look.

A little counting should do it in this situation. East knows from the opening lead that West has four clubs in his hand, so he also knows that declarer has three. Since declarer bid hearts and diamonds, he should have at least nine cards in the red suits. (With four hearts and four diamonds, he would either open one diamond or, if he opened one heart with 2-4-4-3 pattern, rebid in no-trump.)

Putting all of his calculations together, East can place declarer with just one spade, and deduce that a spade shift should be more productive than persevering with clubs. And the spade *king* should be led just in case declarer's singleton spade should turn out to be the queen!

WORKING IT OUT

Assuming declarer can be trusted to play logically, the defenders can draw helpful inferences from the way he handles the dummy. The following is a simple example of how this can be worked out:

```
                    NORTH
                    ♠ 765
                    ♡ Q852
                    ◊ K752
                    ♣ A4
WEST                                    EAST
♠ J942                                  ♠ 103
♡ 4                                     ♡ 973
◊ QJ108                                 ◊ A964
♣ QJ83                                  ♣ 10972
                    SOUTH
                    ♠ AKQ8
                    ♡ AKJ106
                    ◊ 3
                    ♣ K65
```

WEST	NORTH	EAST	SOUTH
			1H
Pass	2H	Pass	2S
Pass	4H	Pass	4NT
Pass	5D	Pass	6H
All Pass			

West leads the queen of diamonds, winning, and continues with the jack. Declarer ruffs and plays the club ace, club king, and another club, ruffing in dummy. He then runs off all his trumps. On the last one West has to throw either a spade or the queen of clubs.

It is an easy problem—declarer cannot have another club, or else he simply would have ruffed it in dummy. West can safely discard the club queen and save his precious spades.

DECEPTION

Declarer may have one edge in deceptive play—he need not worry about fatally misleading a partner. But he certainly has no monopoly on deception.

```
                    NORTH
                    ♠ A Q 10 3
                    ♡ J 4
                    ◇ K J 9 2
                    ♣ J 5 4
        WEST                            EAST
        ♠ K 7 6                         ♠ 8 5 4
        ♡ 9 7 2                         ♡ K Q 10 8 3
        ◇ 7 6 5                         ◇ A Q 4
        ♣ 10 9 8 7                      ♣ 6 2
                    SOUTH
                    ♠ J 9 2
                    ♡ A 6 5
                    ◇ 10 8 3
                    ♣ A K Q 3
```

WEST	NORTH	EAST	SOUTH
			1C
Pass	1S	Pass	1NT
Pass	3NT	All Pass	

West starts with the ten of clubs, which goes to declarer's queen. Declarer counts only six top tricks, but a successful finesse in either diamonds or spades will give him nine. To keep his options open, he tries the diamonds first, leading the eight and finessing. If this loses to East's queen and a heart comes back, declarer plans to fall back on the spade finesse.

East, for his part, can tell that any spade finesse declarer tries will work, so he wants to make declarer think he is on the right track in diamonds. He wins the first diamond with the *ace* and returns the king of hearts.

Now declarer thinks the contract is in the bag. He wins the heart ace and leads the ten of diamonds for another finesse, expecting to take four clubs, three diamonds, a heart and a spade. But East, the dog, produces the diamond queen and cashes four heart tricks to set the contract two.

Appendix

The Winning Records of Oswald and James Jacoby 1931–1986

OSWALD JACOBY (1902–1984)

World Championships

World Team Championship, 1935
Captain, U.S. World Championship Team, 1970, 1971

North American Championships

Spingold Knockout Teams, 1934, 1936, 1938, 1939, 1945, 1950, 1959
Vanderbilt Knockout Teams, 1931, 1934, 1935, 1937, 1938, 1946, 1965
Reisinger Board-a-Match Teams, 1955, 1983
Master Individual, 1935
Master Mixed Teams, 1968
Life Master Pairs, 1936
Men's Teams, 1952, 1959
Open Pairs, 1935, 1960, 1964
Men's Pairs, 1934, 1939, 1949

Runner-up in these and other events innumerable times.

JAMES JACOBY (b. 1933)

World Championships

World Team Championship, 1970, 1971

North American Championships

Spingold Knockout Teams, 1969
Vanderbilt Knockout Teams, 1965, 1967, 1971, 1981
Reisinger Board-a-Match Teams, 1955, 1970, 1977
Grand National Teams, 1981, 1986
Master Mixed Teams, 1968
Men's Teams, 1968, 1972, 1973
Men's Pairs, 1956
North American Swiss Teams, 1985

Runner-up many times in World Championship and North American Championship events.

Index